THE PLAYS OF JOHN OSBORNE

THE PLAYS
OF
JOHN OSBORNE

An Assessment

SIMON TRUSSLER

LONDON
VICTOR GOLLANCZ LTD
1969

Printed in Great Britain by
The Camelot Press Ltd., London and Southampton

To

GLENDA

with love

Contents

Acknowledgements

Extracts from *Look Back in Anger* are reprinted here by kind permission of John Osborne and Messrs Faber and Faber, and extracts from John Osborne's other plays by kind permission of the author and David Higham Associates. The page references in the text are to both the hard-cover and paperback editions of the plays published by Faber and Faber.

My thanks are also due to Wendy Slemen and Mary Taylor for transforming successive drafts into typescript, to Giles Gordon of Victor Gollancz Ltd for constructive criticisms and forbearance, and to my wife, Glenda, and all those friends and students who have helped me to form or to defend opinions for which the responsibility remains, of course, my own.

INTRODUCTION

Introduction

FIRST NIGHT NOTICES and gobbets of gossip apart, the writer most intimately associated with the new-wave drama has been subjected to scant critical scrutiny. For John Osborne repels criticism almost as strongly as he declares himself repelled by critics. Exegesis of Harold Pinter's smaller but densely-textured output is, on the other hand, a booming academic industry: and the valedictory issue of the influential drama magazine *Encore* was entirely given over to a reassessment of John Arden's work. Osborne's relative neglect—even by critics who would readily admit his claim to consideration alongside those fellow front-runners—is probably due as much to an unfashionable forthrightness in his plays as to his undisguised contempt for critics. Thus, his works offer no such tempting ambiguities or pregnant pauses as Pinter's: neither is his craftsmanship so careful or his sectional following so devoted as Arden's. His plays, good and bad alike, appeal to the emotions rather than the intellect. Formulated and sprawling on the critic's pin, they have a discomfiting habit of exploding in his face, spattering him with loose entrails that resist being forced back into their specimen cases.

All too often, the biographical fallacy has proved an alternative funk-hole: and the resultant assumption that Osborne is to be identified with each of his heroes in turn, from George Dillon to the dominating Laurie of *The Hotel in Amsterdam*, has probably been the most persistent obstacle to a better understanding of his work. The fact that both George and Laurie are writers—the first a failure, the second an overtaxed success—makes the fallacy all the more tempting. So too does the gradual ascent in social strata, from the lower depths of *Look Back in Anger* to the intellectual affluence of *Amsterdam*. Now of course Osborne *has* drawn upon and transmuted personal experience. All art is a superior form of sublimation: but fruitful sublimation also involves distortion —or "organised evasion", as Osborne himself has put it.[1] In any case, such fragments of autobiography as may be hidden in his works are for his future biographers to ferret out. The critic's concern must be with the "given" work of art, to which the obsessions and even the intentions of the artist are of no more than marginal interest. And among all forms which have their origins in the written word, the drama is the most public of public properties: therefore it is as a work to which Osborne can claim paternity but not sole guardianship that I intend to treat each of his plays.

The arrangement of my commentary is chronological. There are, inevitably, themes and interests which recur from play to play, but these have, in the main, been left as loose-ends—hopefully albeit summarily tied together in my concluding chapter. It is only there that I have hazarded an interim assessment of Osborne's status as a dramatist, and of his present strengths and weaknesses. Of course, such an assessment isn't really a "conclusion" at all, and because it is necessarily tentative it is also short. At this stage of Osborne's career it seemed most sensible to consider his work on a play-by-play basis, and to avoid overmuch discussion of his "development". At present he is an *ad hoc* playwright, with no predetermined sense of direction. If he ever does plot a more consistent course, his work will probably become easier to interpret—but a lot less interesting.

My penultimate chapter is of a supplementary rather than

a complementary nature. It attempts to dispose of such of Osborne's ventures into non-theatrical polemics as demand to be noticed—but which would project the playwright over-forcefully into his plays if they were cited too insistently as sources for the illumination of individual works. For the record, too, a factual chronology of Osborne's life will be found among the appendices—in which are also collected together the cast-lists and credits of London productions of his plays. And finally there is a bibliography of material by and about the writer. The appearance of John Russell Taylor's *Casebook* on *Look Back in Anger*[2] as the present work was going to press has enabled me to give this alternative and readily accessible source of much material: but its contents have also been of some selfish comfort, in confirming that the body of available criticism, even of this most seminal of Osborne's plays, is relatively scant and sometimes of no more than peripheral interest.

An explanation is due for my failure to discuss the plays-in-production. I have, in fact, seen all but one of the plays discussed in this book on the stage, and in most cases their original London productions—in early days as a squatter in the Royal Court's miniscule but matey upper-circle, latterly from the comfort of *Tribune's* press-seats further down. In consequence, I *have* reviewed most of the plays in the immediacy of their productions—either in obscure student journals, or in my columns in *Tribune* and the *Tulane Drama Review*. I am laying claim to such credentials because the analyses which follow are *not* reviews of a particular director's rendering of a play, but exercises in a kind of criticism that attempts to combine the crafts of the "literary" and the "dramatic" critic. Perhaps the best description of my intended approach is dramaturgical—at least, I can think of no less pretentious-sounding word to describe the discussion of playtexts as the raw-material of productions, rather than as the finished-products which are the business of the student of drama-as-literature.

It is thus the *lasting* potential of the plays, as aspirants to a place in any director's platonic repertory, that has concerned me—and not the excellences or flaws of this or that performance in this or that theatre. Of course, such qualities or defects may be symptomatic of abiding strengths or weaknesses in a script, and I hope I have recognised such symptoms: but they are just as likely to reflect a compromise dictated by economics, or a hungover performance after a first-night party. I ask, in short, that this book be judged not as a study of the theatrical conditions which influenced any particular production, but as a commentary on those features of each script which are likely to prove of interest to the director of any prospective revival. It is, then, as works for the theatre, not as printed texts, that I have discussed each play: and it is because I can claim no experience as a critic of the cinema that I have avoided more than incidental references to the film versions of certain of the plays, or to the printed script of Osborne's screenplay of *Tom Jones*.

I have worked brief synopses of plots into each chapter, but these are intended to jog memories rather than to substitute summary for substance. It is for this reason that I have given page-references to the texts of the plays, as published by Faber and Faber, in square-brackets immediately after each quotation or allusion: this is a bit unsightly, but it should enable the reader to follow my argument in close conjunction with his set of playscripts, and not to be forced scuttling to footnotes or the back of the book in order to correlate the two. References other than those to the plays have been kept to a minimum: these are indicated by superior numerals, and they *have* been tucked away in an appendix for the benefit of anyone who wishes to identify this or that source more fully— but for the lesser distraction of the general reader, who is unlikely to have a file of *The Times Literary Supplement* or *The Hudson Review* or whatever conveniently to hand.

The book thus sets out to be as much a companion to Osborne's plays as a criticism of them, and it is my hope that my ideas will set off arguments and disagreements rather than assert themselves as definitive. This they can scarcely be, for they are almost invariably gropings in the dark of territory that has never before been explored in depth: and as such they are as tentative as any ideas unmodified by an existing tradition of informed criticism must invariably be. Maybe this book will help to stimulate a serious critical debate about Osborne—even if it serves only negatively as a sounding-board for dissent.

With a dozen plays in about as many working years to his credit, Osborne has not only established his staying-power as a dramatist—a capacity for endurance which some of his earliest critics doubted[3]—but written enough, both in quantity and quality, for this kind of provisional assessment to be attempted. It is because my assessment *is* no more than provisional that I have probably erred towards over-criticism rather than over-kindness in the following chapters. Osborne is just about in the prime of life, and the plays of his later maturity may well be his best. At present, he is still an *instinctive* craftsman, though he is becoming a much more conscious dialectician—an assertion which anticipates its proof, because I want at this stage to clarify one of my underlying intentions. This is neither to praise nor to bury Osborne, but to offer as constructive a critique as possible of a dramatist whose career should have a lengthier future than it has a past. In that belief, I offer my own discussion of his first dozen plays—in part a textual analysis, in part a theatrical commentary, and in part a personal interpretation.

THE PLAYS OF JOHN OSBORNE

I

Epitaph for George Dillon

EPITAPH FOR GEORGE DILLON was the second play
Osborne wrote in collaboration with Anthony Creighton,
and it has proved to be a sole survivor among five prentice
pieces—the only one that the dramatist has chosen to re-
furbish for the West End, or to admit into the printed canon
of his work.[4] The present text is the end-product of at least
two stages of revision: and even the play's title was for a
time abbreviated into *George Dillon* before it reverted to its
first and fuller form. The purpose of the structural changes
which took place between the play's limited season at the
Royal Court in February 1958 and its brief transfer to the
Comedy Theatre a few months later was to iron out three
sequences in flashback which had come under heavy critical
fire: but neither the nature nor the extent of the alterations
made *before* the first production is certain. Neither, for that
matter, is the extent of Anthony Creighton's share in the
play—though it has been widely assumed that Osborne
contributed those episodes which are rooted in the rhetoric
of Dillon himself, and that Creighton filled-out the more
discursive family scenes. Certainly, *Epitaph for George Dillon*
remains the only one of Osborne's extant plays over which
any hand but his own has poised a pen: and, more to the
point, it is his only work to depend so absolutely on the
theatrical conventions which prevailed in the early nineteen-
fifties.

But it is in more than merely pedantic mood that I want to
justify my treatment of *Epitaph for George Dillon* as a first play.

Robert Brustein, reviewing its New York production, was not alone in comparing the piece favourably with *Look Back in Anger* and *The Entertainer*—even citing it as evidence that Osborne was a "developing artist . . . not simply an *enfant terrible*".[5] And such a sense of artistic advance as Brustein discerned might have justified the play's promotion in my own running-order. But the impression I have actually formed of *Epitaph for George Dillon*—as a play uncertain in construction and casual in characterisation—will make it not only more convenient but more equitable to ignore all but the most obtrusive marks of revision, and to treat it as the earliest work we possess from Osborne's hands.

Epitaph for George Dillon is set "in the home of the Elliot family just outside London". [10] The only hint of a more precise location is Mrs Elliot's gratuitous remark that Targon Wood Station is nearer than Pelham Junction— a blatant pseudonymity of *locale* reminiscent of a period when all the best people in plays lived in Loamshire. [30] The Elliots are by no means the best people, however. They are of the lower-middle classes: but the transposition of upper-crust comedy conventions into a drama about the pettiest of the bourgeoisie is recurrent. In her owner-occupied semi, Mrs Elliot—the only character never addressed by her Christian name—exerts a benevolent but firm matriarchy over her husband Percy, her two daughters Norah and Josie, and her younger, divorced sister Ruth. The whole family, with one significant exception, commute daily to unspecified but evidently routine employments. George Dillon, however, is unrelated, and temperamentally un-employed: he acts infrequently, and tries to write. His intrusion into the Elliot household—an event occupying the play's first act—is explained somewhat cursorily as a symp-tom of Mrs Elliot's failure to adjust to the wartime death of a son, and of her consequent need to succour a substitute. Upon her vicarious charity George Dillon therefore proceeds to batten.

The play's domestic interior, as described in Osborne's opening direction, [11] suggests, like its mythical suburban whereabouts, a drawing-room comedy of the welfare state. There are even french-windows: but they look out "on to a small back garden", not a tennis court. And the utility furniture, the tinted wedding-group, the bowl of pre-plastic but everlasting flowers, the painting of ducks in flight—all point to the philistinism of Woolworth's rather than of Harrod's. They point, indeed, a little too insistently: there is even a monstrous, rarely utilised cocktail-cabinet, and, standing upon it, "a large china model of an alsatian dog". One invisible wall divides the sitting-room from the hall, and a stairway ascends beyond the audience's view. In this single setting the decline of George Dillon runs its course, separated out into the customary three acts.

The first is mainly expository. The second contains what Kenneth Tynan in his original review, in February 1958, described as "a long duologue which in terms of human contact and mutual exploration is better than anything in Mr Osborne's later unaided works".[6] This duologue is between George and Ruth, who has just fallen out of love with a self-pitying artist much like—overmuch like—Dillon himself. She has also, irrelevantly, just resigned from the Communist Party. The second act constitutes the main "development" of the action, concluding—as it does rather abruptly—with George jumping into bed with Josie. Of course—and the consequence, for all its hedging-about with irony, underlines the technical immaturity of the piece—the girl gets pregnant. And the third act—pausing briefly to enable George to go down, like all good romantics, with tuberculosis—witnesses his final surrender to a mediocre marriage, to the comfortable virtues of his prospective mother-in-law, and to the aesthetic values of a pedlar of sex-shows, who persuades George to dirty-up one of his plays.

Epitaph, in short, conforms to a common formal mould: and even its matrimonial climax completes a dramatic circle which is arguably vicious, but which is none the less conventional in its curvature. How many questions Osborne's conclusion begs is suggested by the later *Look Back in Anger*, which has an intellectually unbalanced marriage as its premise rather than its climax, and which resolves only into compromise. Jimmy Porter and Alison are better matched, if anything, than George Dillon and Josie: but in his second play Osborne was concerned to show that life is less neatly segmented than *Epitaph for George Dillon* makes out—as much in its title as in its conclusion.

Paradoxically, it is at once its lack of *human* complexity and a superfluity of *dramatic* complication that flaws the play. Its characters represent ethical absolutes. They embody carefully opposed ways of life, and might be accommodated in a non-naturalistic thinkpiece satisfactorily enough: but they fail even to live up to their own simplicity in an overtly realistic play. For one thing, the very presence of George and Ruth in the Elliot household makes it exceptional of its suburban kind. The Elliots are represented as typical—and yet they are conceived as living in an environment, and within a complex of human relationships, which presuppose their atypicality.

On the evidence of the action, George's outburst against his adopted family in the second act is therefore not only "pretty cheap", as Ruth assesses it, but fundamentally wrong:

Have you looked at them? Have you listened to them? They don't merely act and talk like caricatures, they *are* caricatures! That's what's so terrifying. Put any one of them on a stage, and no one would take them seriously for one minute! They think in clichés, they talk in them, they even feel in them—and, brother, that's an achievement! Their existence is one great cliché that they carry about with them like a snail in his little house—and they live in it and die in it! [58-9]

This is possibly no more than an exercise in self-justification. Dramatically, however, the Elliots do live down to George's estimate of them—although existentially they *must* be more complex than they are allowed to appear. After all, Mrs Elliot has invited a total stranger into her household on the strength of a fancied resemblance to her dead son. She is effectively estranged from her husband, who is a guest in his own home, although her two daughters are separated by fifteen years: so that the imagination boggles at the reconciliatory tumble that went into Josie's conception. In none of these respects are the Elliots representative: and yet they are consistently rendered as caricatures.

Even the family names have a mannered, onomatopoeic ring—for Ruth is strident, Norah is normal and boring, and Josie is rosy and jolly. This youngest daughter is first seen scanning the problems-page of a woman's magazine: and she exudes admiration for jazz and motor-cycles. Mrs Elliot duly despises "them morbid plays" on television. [26] And such habits of mind as are crystallised here echo the easiest kind of intellectual assumptions about philistinism—assumptions which are *themselves* clichés. There is no probing beneath the surface—either of the stock bourgeois image, or of the stock response to it.

The Elliots' way of life—a way of life that should contain its implicit condemnation—also suffers from verbal over-exposure. Thus, I feel sorry for any bit-player cast as the man from the National Assistance Board, who investigates

George's claim for help. "Officialdom relaxing" is how Osborne's stage direction apologises for his exit speech:

> You know, you people are a funny lot. I don't understand you. Look what you do to yourselves. And all for what? What do you get out of it? It beats me. Now take me and my wife. We don't have any worries. I've got my job during the day—secure, pension at the end of it. Mrs Webb is at home, looking after the kiddies—she knows there'll be a pay-packet every Friday. And in the evenings, we sit at home together, or sometimes we'll go out. But we're happy. There's quite a lot to it, you know. . . . What could be better? I ask you? No, you think it over, son. You think it over. [71]

This sort of confessional is not merely out of character, but theatrically inept: it is in flagrant breach of the play's chosen conventions. And there is a similar over-explicitness about the eulogy of Hitler permitted to Barney Evans, the seedy backer of George's play. [77–8] It is not enough that Barney epitomises the small-time impresario, ever ready to defend ruthlessness in his dealings: it is *totalitarian* ruthlessness that Barney has to advocate. It is not to the point that certain businessmen may be prone to just such sympathies— but that in Barney's case such verbalising is made to do all the work, and of an inner Barney to explain the outward bluster there is not a glimpse.

Less obtrusively, but symptomatically, George's first wife —forgotten till the final act—just *has* to be Percy's favourite panellist on a television parlour-game. [90] Ruth, on her first appearance, just *has* to betray her hemmed-in intellectuality by enquiring after the identity of Frankie Vaughan: [17] and her cast-off lover just *has* to get his first novel published and acclaimed a mere three months after their parting.

[85] As for Norah, the dowdying, thirtyish sister, George's assertion that she "doesn't even exist—she's just a hole in the air" [60] has a certain metaphysical aptness. But demonstrably Norah *does* exist: she has to be translated into a living person by a living actress. And an unresisting conformity to a doomed-to-spinsterhood stereotype is all that the text yields by way of interpretive assistance.

One test of the success of naturalistically drawn characters is how well they measure up dramatically to their encapsulated introductions in their creator's stage directions. Josie, we are told, "may be funny at times, but she is never consciously so". [14] And Percy is "small in every sense of the word, with a small man's aggression". [25] Such comments are really more revealing than anything in the action or dialogue that is intended to substantiate them: and actors are accordingly encouraged to develop the character-parts the comments suggest. As George says of the Elliots, they "don't merely act and talk like caricatures, they *are* caricatures"—which as an authorial apology is akin to the storybook heroine's reflection about things like this only happening to story-book heroines.

I have commented on the more peripheral characters first, since their lack of substance otherwise tempts one to discuss them impressionistically, in relation to George—and I don't think that this kind of existence can be accorded them in the play produced. The obvious contrast is with *Inadmissible Evidence*, in which the subservience of the minor characters to Bill Maitland's mental state *is* skilfully suggested. In *Epitaph*, however, George is evidently supposed to exist within an objectively realistic context, and the insufficiency of that context diminishes his own dramatic identity. Worse, Ruth— the single character who does begin to give George a return on his rhetoric—is a puzzlingly hybrid creation. Presumably, in the play's original draft, the issue of her defection from the Communist Party, and of her propensity towards lame-ducks, bulked much larger. As the play stands, however, such personality-traits remain embryonic.

The Ruth of the second act is little more than a mirror-image of George, and, for that matter, of her departed lover. Thus, the latter's farewell note, which Josie reads aloud—and how venerable a Scribean device that now seems—has the distinctive ring of the early, petulant Osborne heroes:

> My dear—You have just left, and I have found that you have left two pounds for me on the desk. . . . Make no mistake—for the money, I'm grateful. But your setting up as a kind of emotional soup kitchen makes me spit. . . . If you had any understanding at all, you would know what a bitter taste this kind of watery gruel must have. This is the Brown Windsor of love all right, and the only fit place for it is the sink. If this is the kind of thing you and your pals would dole out for the proletariat and its poor, grubby artists, you had better think again. I'm just going out for some beer. PS. Was just going to post this, when I thought I would return this watch to you. It seems to be the one thing I have left that you ever gave me. I'd like to think that my returning it would hurt you, but I know it won't. [23]

This bears quoting at length: it is excellent stuff. But it is a homogeneous excellence, as much in George's vein or even in Ruth's own, as in her anonymous lover's.

For such a merging of identities a few self-conscious apologies are offered. Ruth tells George he is "rather like" her former lover, [51] and George accuses her of mouthing second-hand phrases. [63] It is scarcely surprising that at their very first meeting he senses that he has met Ruth somewhere before. "Yes, I had that feeling too," is her reply. [29] But, one feels impelled to ask, so what? Is Ruth's relationship with George narcissistic, or solipsistic, or something? Symbolic it certainly is, at the play's climactic moment—as this Ibsenesque stage-direction, which follows George's submission to the forces of the Elliots, suggests. A mollified Percy

> opens the cocktail cabinet, revealing all its hidden glory. Ruth exits through front door. [93]

This moment has been carefully prepared: the cabinet has even been described by George himself as "some sort of monstrous symbol"—and he demonstrates his independence of whatever it symbolises by sitting down and "playing" the thing, like an end-of-pier piano. [54–5] But although he ponders over what might be kept in it—old razor-blades, perhaps—its mysteries remain concealed until George submits to his fate: then Percy extracts the celebratory sherry, and Ruth simultaneously exits.

Unfortunately, this kind of terribly *significant* level is the only level at which Ruth's relationship with George really works. After their second-act duologue, there is no hint of how its mutual revelations have affected or developed the intimacy between them. In the last act their exchanges are cursory and infrequent, and their parting is no more than an excuse for George to recite his own epitaph:

> Here lies the body of George Dillon, aged thirty-four—or thereabouts—who thought, who hoped, he was that mysterious, ridiculous being called an artist. He never allowed himself one day of peace. He worshipped the physical things of this world, and was betrayed by his own body. He loved also the things of the mind, but his own brain was a cripple from the waist down. He achieved

nothing he set out to do. He made no one happy, no one look up with excitement when he entered the room. He was always troubled with wind round his heart, but he loved no one successfully. He was a bit of a bore, and, frankly, rather useless. But the germs loved him. . . . Even his sentimental epitaph is probably a pastiche of someone or other, but he doesn't quite know who. And, in the end, it doesn't really matter. [87]

At such moments, when George is indulging in soliloquies of self-pity, one begins to know him. But this is the character who has been described on his first entrance as displaying "a mercurial, ironic passion, lethargy, offensiveness, blatant sincerity and a mentally picaresque dishonesty—sometimes almost all of these at the same time". [29] And we seldom sense the complication here suggested, because George exists in a separate, altogether solider dimension than the Elliots, whose simplicity condemns him to emote in a vacuum.

Consider just one moment when a complication is evidently intended. George is an inveterate predator: and his intimacy with Ruth really begins at the moment she presents him with a watch—her former lover's, of course—which George describes as "the nicest present I've had". [52] Now he chooses *precisely* the same words to describe the gift of a portable typewriter which consummates, as it were, his alliance with the Elliots. [92] The coincidence in phraseology, unless it is clumsily coincidental, must be purposeful: and yet it connects with nothing. Is the implication that George's responses are as commonplace as those of the Elliots? Perhaps: but on this evidence they are certainly not the responses of a "walking confliction". [29] Any such "confliction" is controlled self-consciously: it is expressed when George switches on the rhetoric. At other times—on his first arrival, or during the interview with the Assistance Board man—he is a far less interesting person, and not so very ill-adapted to the Elliot menage.

This raises the issue of George's own responsibility for his eventual absorption. Authorially, Osborne neither praises nor condemns his hero, and this is as it should be. But the issue is never given much vitality: for if Ruth serves as a mirror for narcissus, the rest of the family lack even such reflected reality. They exist only to personify ethical values which George and—in this case, at least—his creator detest. Characters from outside the family make their brief appearances for a similar purpose. Mr Webb of the Assistance Board radiates bureaucratic smugness and homespun virtue, as does Barney Evans the inverted values of admass culture: and as Geoffrey Colwyn-Stuart—a revivalist acquaintance of Mrs Elliot's, whose function is to get the good lady out of the way for the second act—embodies benign religiosity.

It doesn't so much matter that of these three only Barney contributes anything positive to the progress of the plot: but it does matter that they too fail to give dramatic counterpoint to the conflict within George himself. Colwyn-Stuart has some nicely-turned speeches, very much catching the style of the off-duty cleric: but these succeed in identifying him even more completely with his representative role. Thus, George's declared belief that "the truth is a caricature" [61] is confirmed, and never complicated, by what he experiences: there is nothing to throw either the experience or the self-pity it induces into relief.

Very much in the manner of a maker of well-made plays, Osborne has thus engineered a confrontation of values which is *likely* to generate conflict—and then he has fought shy of that conflict. The bones of such structuring protrude through the emaciated flesh of the dramatic action. Weaknesses in plotting abound—and of these perhaps the most blatant is George's tuberculosis. It effects nothing, changes nothing: and if it is meant to enhance our sympathy for George, it does so in the most obvious and commonplace way. The hospitalised recovery, however, permits a necessary pause. It gives Josie not only a good curtain-line, but time to get more pregnant. And it allows Percy time to research into his potential son-in-law's past, thereby justifying his job as an investigator of creditworthiness: for in the course of this unlikely duty, he stumbles upon the existence of George's separated wife. The discovery builds up an orthodox sort of suspense, which falls bathetically flat upon George's casual assertion—which is accepted with equal casualness—that a divorce can readily be procured. [90] The whole inconsequential business merely prompts one to wonder what George would have done if Percy *hadn't* been employed by a credit-clearance firm: committed bigamy, presumably.

Other weaknesses of construction are of a kind common to most "well-made" plays, and are usually intended to facilitate the business of exposition. The unlikeliness of Mrs Elliot's failure to mention George's impending arrival till he's practically on the doorstep, and the coincidence of his losing his job on the same day, are explicable in the interests of a tightly-knit time structure. The returned watch in the first act prepares the ground, both functionally and symbolically, for Ruth's gift to George in the second. Such are the faults of a young dramatist working in an outmoded genre, and still uncertain about handling the raw material of his plot. Consider, in such a light, this brief exchange:

MRS ELLIOT: You do look tired, I must say.
RUTH: Oh, I'm better now. Josie gave her *Auntie* a cup of tea.
MRS ELLIOT: You always hate her calling you Auntie don't

you. What can you expect dear when that's what you are? [18]

This makes several points: that Ruth is worried about her age, and about appearing aged to others; that she is, indeed, Josie's aunt, and not her elder sister—and that Josie relishes reminding her of the fact. But how clumsily the points are made—clumsily not in terms of hack playmongering, but in terms of one's expectations of Osborne. And even his sense of the spoken word occasionally lets him down. At one point in the second-act duologue, George is made to remark:

It's like living in one of those really bad suitable-for-all-the-family comedies they do all the year round in weekly rep. in Wigan. [60]

The final phrase is as irritating to the tongue as to the intelligence. It seeks an automatic response to the place-name, moreover, in the very process of offering a selfconscious apology for the resemblance of the unfolding action to that of an inferior domestic farce.

There is a similar sense of misplaced effort in the working-towards a strong curtain-line for each act or scene. Only the final curtain is really successful, and this is taken as slowly as its conviction warrants. The earlier quick-curtains are all more or less contrived, and that to the penultimate scene is reminiscent of the triply-extended tags of soap-opera:

JOSIE: Oh, my God. Auntie Ruth! What's going to happen? What about me?
RUTH: You?
JOSIE: Yes, that's what I want to know—what's going to happen to me? [80]

B

Comment would be superfluous. On the other hand, there are rare moments when the striving for rhetorical effect is forgotten, and the dialogue rings suddenly true:

> RUTH: Mr Dillon has arrived, Kate.
> MRS ELLIOT: Oh, good. You found your way all right, then? Glad you remembered it was Targon Wood station you had to get out at—most people think Pelham Junction is nearer, but it isn't really. I didn't hear you ring the bell. I expect you're hungry, aren't you? Would you like a wash before supper? Bring your things up. . . . I'll show you where your room is and where you can find the toilet. [30]

But for those obtrusively invented names, and—perhaps significantly—at a moment when nothing is really being said, Mrs Elliot's lines are allowed to express individuality, not dramatic necessity: and her stream of embarrassed consciousness, in which speech becomes no more than a preventive to silence, couldn't be more in character. In fact, Mrs Elliot's inconsequential stabs at politeness tell an audience more about the choice which is to confront George Dillon than most of his own verbalised agonies.

It is an indication of the play's weakness that what *Epitaph* is really *about* thus tends to emerge only negatively from an analysis of its characterisation and its construction. Thematically, it is a bunch of loose ends. It is ostensibly concerned with the progress of the artist as a young philistine: yet the action adds up only to the *how* of this progress, scarcely even hinting at the *why*—which is bound up with Mrs Elliot's past, Ruth's past, George's past. Beyond suggesting a connection between her blind affection for George and the loss of her own son—a perfunctory gesture, as it were, to paperbacked psychology—Osborne fills out Mrs Elliot hardly at all. Ruth he delivers over as a foil to George, though occasional hints of an independent existence are wafted into their second-act confrontation—this, for instance, on her abandonment of the Communist Party:

> Seventeen years. It's rather like walking out on a lover. All over, finished, kaput. He hardly listened to my explanation—just sat there with a sneer all over his face. He didn't even have the manners to get up and show me out. I think that's what I've hated most of all, all these years—the sheer, damned bad manners of the lot of them. [50]

"Farther left you go, the worse the manners seem to get," replies George, as exposition descends into not very accurate generalisation. And to explain such references as the untrimmed leftovers of an earlier draft is not to excuse them. The play must perforce be judged as Osborne and Creighton allowed it to reach the stage.

As such, it is a muddle—in which all kinds of recognisably Osbornian themes float among dramatic driftwood. There is the theme of George's mother-worship—foreshadowing Jimmy Porter's deification of Hugh's mother in *Look Back in Anger,* and in rather the same lushly nostalgic tones:

> We often used to go out together—she enjoyed that more than anything. She'd pay for the lot: drinks, meals, cinemas—even the bus fares. When the conductor came up the stairs, I would always grope in my pockets. And my mother would bring out her purse, and push my empty, fumbling hands away. "It's all right, dear. I've got change." I used to wonder whether perhaps there might come just *one* day when it might not have to happen. When I might actually have that two shillings or half-crown in

> my pocket. But it always did. It had become a liturgy. We
> went through it the last time we went out together—on my
> thirtieth birthday. [52]

Now this is precisely the kind of maternal generosity which
Mrs Elliot also lavishes on her substitute-son. Is *this* what
draws George into the family bosom—or does he really
relish the remembered experience as an excuse for wallowing
in nostalgia, not for its actuality?

There's no means of telling: the thread is severed as
abruptly as it is woven into the play. But it's notable that we
learn far more of George's mother from this speech than we
ever learn of his *wife*—though one senses that their marriage
was, like Jimmy Porter's, hypergamous. Is it a compensatory
need to marry beneath himself that now draws George to
Josie's animal warmth? Or the need for a narcissistic mirror
tinted more rosily than Ruth's? The questions are insistent:
not because a naturalistic playwright has any obligation to
etherise his characters and allocate them labels in a psychological casebook, but because *Epitaph for George Dillon* adds up
to little more than such a casebook—its labels distributed,
sometimes at random, among its characters. The little more
it *does* offer—though this is seminally vital—is the dignity
George himself achieves: not in his filial or his sexual relationships, but in his language.

Significantly, George is not only an actor, but an actor
playing at being an actor:

> I think I play "scornful" parts—anyone a bit loud-
> mouthed, around my height, preferably rough and dirty,
> with a furnace roaring in his belly. The rougher and
> dirtier the better. [53]

This might very well *be* Jimmy Porter: but it is no more than

George Dillon's chosen persona. And that persona he creates verbally—in the piling-up of phrases which culminate only in an assertive afterthought, or in the repetitive rhythms of some self-protective music-hall patter. George is always at two removes from his real-life audience: he exists not only as a character in a play, but as a character playing a character. There is even a Pirandellian air at times to his relationship with his actual audience, as it listens, for example, to George describing his lifelong battle against—an audience.

> I attract hostility. I seem to be on heat for it. Whenever I step out on to those boards—immediately, from the very first moment I show my face—I know I've got to fight almost every one of those people in the auditorium. Right from the stalls to the gallery, to the Vestal Virgins in the boxes! My God, it's a gladiatorial combat! Me against Them! Me and mighty Them! Oh, I may win some of them over. Sometimes it's a half maybe, sometimes a third, sometimes it's not even a quarter. But I *do* beat them down. I beat them down! And even in the hatred of the majority, there's a kind of triumph because I know that, although they'd never admit it, they secretly respect me. [56–7]

Ruth is a "good audience" for George precisely in the theatrical rather than the conversational sense, for his rhetoric works isolatively, not reciprocally. Thus, we don't need George's ironic recollection of this advice from Barney Evans to a budding playwright to register its prophetic overtones:

> BARNEY: You know, that's a very good idea—getting the girl in the family way.

GEORGE: You think so?
BARNEY: Never fails. Get someone in the family way in the Third Act—you're half-way there. [76–7]

Josie is duly got in the family way in the third act—but Barney's prophecy strikes one as apologetic rather than ironic, for it goes beyond the bounds of the naturalistic conventions which confine the girl. And one's sense of clumsiness is only confirmed by George's later explication of the irony. [86] The fact remains that the scornful, sophisticated George Dillon *has* fallen into the trap set by so many dramatists for so many heroes and villains, of getting a blushing virgin in the family way in the final act.

Any well-trained audience might have known it, of course, as soon as the second-act curtain fell on Percy watching George and Josie's guilty flight upstairs:

RUTH: Why, Percy, how long have you been there?
PERCY: Long enough, I think. Quite long enough. [67]

Again, the double-barrelled verbiage of soap-opera raises an expectation which is justified by the event. Such devices are, as it were, technical corollaries to the emotional and intellectual insufficiency of *Epitaph for George Dillon*. The play's theme does foreshadow Osborne's later forays into sectors of the class-war ignored by his predecessors, just as George's spleen bears occasional tidings of Jimmy Porter's wrath to come. But his *Epitaph*, for all its profusion of Osbornian motifs, seems best forgiven as an apprentice work unwisely resurrected—and half-heartedly revised—in its author's hour of better-deserved success.

Even to have discussed it at such length has perhaps been unfair. I have done so in part to elaborate the very weaknesses of the drawing-room family dramas whose conventions

Osborne tried and failed to adapt, but was very soon to transcend—and partly in an attempt to remedy an overrating of the play by critics who preferred its well-made shadow to such looser and baggier but thoroughly dramatic substance as *Look Back in Anger* had to offer.

2

Look Back in Anger

LOOK BACK IN ANGER is at once a play and a myth—a text realisable upon a stage, and an unrealisable ideal in a platonic repertory. Like *Hamlet*, its name and its supposed theme are recognised instantly by many more people than have ever seen a production or read a script: and even the date of its first performance, on 8th May 1956, is beginning to be cited by the esoteric with the kind of awe otherwise reserved for allusions to the traumatic opening night of *Ubu Roi*. Indeed, the play is commonly assigned a seminal responsibility for the flowering of the new English drama analogous to Jarry's grandpaternal fostering of the theatre of the absurd.

This kind of historical embalming has obvious dangers: but it is not altogether possible or even desirable to separate the resultant myth from the reality. A good play, like any major work of art, accretes associations and spawns its own canon of critical commonplaces: and these may nourish or they may blur one's conception of the "given" text, but they cannot, for better or worse, be ignored. So *Look Back in Anger* has long ceased to be its author's personal property. It is necessary to emphasise this point, because it modifies to some extent the force of Osborne's objections to his army of interpreters: for example, that they have chosen to understand Jimmy Porter's outbursts against his wife, his friends, and society in general—outbursts which occupy a substantial proportion of the play—too simply and too superficially.

This, for example, is the playwright's own comment on one of his hero's most persistently mythologised claims, that "there aren't any good, brave causes left".

> Immediately they heard this, all the shallow heads with their savage thirst for trimmed-off explanations got to work on it, and they had enough new symbols to play about with happily and fill their columns for half a year. They believed him, just as some believed Archie Rice when he said: "I don't feel a thing" or "I may be an old pouf, but I'm not right-wing." They were incapable of recognising the texture of ordinary despair, the way it expresses itself in rhetoric and gestures that may perhaps look shabby, but are seldom simple. It is too simple to say that Jimmy Porter himself believed that there were no good, brave causes left, any more than Archie didn't feel a thing.[7]

"Gestures that may perhaps look shabby, but are seldom simple." *Look Back in Anger* is full of them: and they *have* been simplified.

Now in so far as the simplifications have been thrown back into Osborne's teeth—to illustrate his guilt by association with the angry young men, or to support the related assumption that his own opinions are synonymous with those of his hero—they must certainly be denied and resisted. But in one sense the simplifications are a vital and valid aspect of any response to the play: because one emerges from a first acquaintance with it as if from the unwonted exercise of an ill-conditioned body—less concerned with the analysis of particular pains than with a sort of generalised ache. After numbing an audience into such a state, it's not altogether fair for Osborne to complain that his critics have been insufficiently subtle in identifying their reactions: for it was, after all, the playwright himself who suggested that in *Look Back in Anger* he was chiefly concerned to "make people feel, to give them lessons in feeling". True, he admitted that there was time enough to "think afterwards".[8] But feelings tend to be verbalised less subtly than they are assimilated—as Osborne himself, in his more polemical moods, has amply demonstrated. And so the mythical Jimmy Porter, the rebel without good cause, was born.

Baldly stated, the theme of *Look Back in Anger* is familiar enough. Jimmy and Alison's marriage, rapidly breaking down in spite of a certain shared affection and the good offices of the even-tempered Cliff, finally cracks under the strain of Jimmy's continuous verbal onslaughts. His brief, incongruous affair with Alison's friend Helena fails to survive his wife's abject return, and the couple settle down to make the best of the mutual fantasy that protects them as much from each other as from the world. Superficially, then, *Look Back in Anger* amounts to a variation on the eternal-triangular theme, in which the wife wins out over the other woman and the wreck of a marriage is somehow salvaged. And yet, germinating within this well-tended plot, is said to have lain the seed not only of a dramatic renaissance, but of an influential attitude towards life itself: and at least the relative straightforwardness of his story-line did give Osborne a chance he denied himself in *Epitaph for George Dillon* for a really close look at his characters. His play is much richer in fruitful ambiguities as a consequence. But a search for these subtleties seldom leads to the better-trodden critical commonplaces: and still less does it midwife an angry young man, bearing a striking resemblance to his creator, protesting into the world.

It does, admittedly, suggest that *Look Back in Anger* is thoroughly autobiographical in one respect—its hero's entrenched engagement in the war of the classes. In *Epitaph for George Dillon*, the battle was not so much one between classes as within a particular class—the nondescript ranges of the lower middle class. Dillon was of the bourgeoisie— as his final, voluntary incarceration in its bosom confirmed. But Jimmy Porter is self-consciously proletarian— and self-protectively proud of it. Osborne's grandfather— whom he describes in the credo contributed to *Declaration* with an affection he rarely evinces towards cricket-playing admirers of Lord Beaverbrook[9]—was a shabby-genteel Edwardian (such as Alison's father in *Look Back in Anger*, and such as Billy Rice in *The Entertainer*). But the shabbiness apparently triumphed over the gentility, and Osborne's immediate family worked hard and long for their livings. The kind of puritanism such a background often breeds—a social rather than a sexual puritanism—is perhaps at the core of Jimmy Porter's character: and the present critic hastens to add that he writes as a working-class-bred social puritan, not as a sociologist.

There is, too, a related sense of *nostalgia* pervading Jimmy's rhetoric, which helps stylistically to account for its constant, associative back-tracking. But this has been commented on often enough. It needs not so much definition as a fuller study of its implications: in brief, however, it is less a nostalgia for past experience than for denied experience —for Colonel Redfern's "long, cool evenings up in the hills, everything purple and golden". For a world which "looked like going on for ever". [68] These are Redfern's own words: but they closely echo Jimmy's earlier evocation of a time of "home-made cakes and croquet, bright ideas, bright uniforms".

Always the same picture: high summer, the long days in the sun, slim volumes of verse, crisp linen, the smell of starch. What a romantic picture. Phoney, too, of course.

It must have rained sometimes. Still, even I regret it, phoney or not. If you've no world of your own, it's rather pleasant to regret the passing of someone else's. I must be getting sentimental. [17]

Jimmy *is* sentimental, of course—profoundly so. And his sense of emotional loss is felt as much by Alison as by her husband—but is never shared between them:

I keep looking back as far as I remember, and I can't think what it was to feel young, really young. Jimmy said the same thing to me the other day. I pretended not to be listening—because I knew that would hurt him, I suppose. And—of course—he got savage, like tonight. But I knew just what he meant. I suppose it would have been so easy to say "Yes, darling, I know just what you mean. I know what you're feeling". (*Shrugs.*) It's those easy things that seem to be so impossible with us. [28]

I don't think it has been remarked that it is in this speech of Alison's that the only explicit reference to *looking back*, other than in the play's title, is made: and the piece is really much more about the impotent anger induced by such an intangible yet irreparable personal loss than it is about the objective anger engendered by the "good, brave causes". Ironically, it is a product equally of Jimmy's proletarian and Alison's upper-class upbringing—and hence the certain incongruity of Jimmy's simultaneous feelings of identification with the working-classes and the aristocracy, for he is less in search of a particular background than of a lost innocence and assurance which both seemed to share.

Their common loss has vitally diminished the marriage of Alison and Jimmy: and it has rendered them sexually inarticulate. Their bears-and-squirrels game is a brave attempt to compensate for this failure by means of an extended metaphor which is tactile as well as verbal: and as we witness the game developing in the play, it is, unexpectedly, not in the least embarrassing—or, as Helena asserts, fey [47]—but strangely fragile and moving. As a form of conventionalised sexual play it has an undoubted dignity of its own—for, as Osborne himself has argued[10], such a mutual perpetuation of a fantasy-level of experience can be a sophisticated form of sexual communication.

This is true as far as it goes: but the gulf which separates them ensures that it is the *only* level on which Jimmy and Alison's marriage really works—and their fantasy is therefore compensatory rather than complementary. Now this, surely, suggests what the play is about—or what it *was* about, before the myth-makers got to work: it explores, within a formally unexceptionable framework, a particular kind of sexual relationship, the incidental frustrations of which (expressed in Jimmy's outbursts about everything *but* his feelings towards his wife) just happened to set off or coincide with a theatrical chain-reaction. Why this happened may emerge from a closer study of the play's construction, and of the complicated emotional processes of its central characters.

Like *Epitaph for George Dillon*, *Look Back in Anger* is built along traditional lines. It has three acts, and specifies a single domestic interior: and although this setting is no longer a drawing-room, but a more or less squalid attic flat, Osborne still relies, perhaps instinctively, on the conventions of the well-made play. There is, however, a considerable advance in technical assurance. Most of the necessary first-act exposition, for example, is got across via the self-pitying grumbles of Jimmy against the alleged insensitivity of Alison and Cliff: but these grumbles are more than technically functional, in so far as they characterise Jimmy's habit of drawing heavily on his past for the raw materials of his rhetoric—and, indeed, his tendency to repeat himself. They also serve to suggest the taut relationship between husband and wife, and the casual, catalytic function of Cliff, partner in Jimmy's "business", who has become a sort of buffer-state between the disputed boundaries of the marriage. Thus is established the paradox of a university graduate who has chosen to retreat to a provincial garret and to make his living running a sweet-stall.

To accommodate Jimmy's verbosity, the action begins on an occasion which is necessarily static—an English Sunday afternoon. Much of the sub-Chekhovian dialogue this occasion inspires is reminiscent of well-wrought situation comedy: and it's worth recalling that one of the vintage *Hancock's Half Hours* tackled precisely the same theme of sabbatical boredom, in not dissimilar terms. Of course, Jimmy's self-employment dictates that the action *must* occur either on Sundays or after business-hours—and this does heighten rather misleadingly the impression of mutually-irritant domestic claustrophobia. Heightened or not, however, it is rendered forcefully enough: and in the process the Sunday papers, Alison's ironing board and, of course, "those bloody bells", [25] serve as verbal props for bored backchat —though Jimmy's invariably euphemistic description of the *Sunday Times* or *The Observer* as 'the other posh one" [13] adheres disconcertingly to the convention that all stage newspapers must be pseudonymous *Daily Globes*, just as *Epitaph* was unwilling to retreat from a sort of suburban Loamshire.

It is a far more technically mature Osborne, however, who dares to open his first and third acts in identical settings— Helena merely succeeding Alison at the ironing board, and Alison instead of Helena disrupting the domesticity. This looking-glass effect not only succeeds theatrically, but shapes the action into a closed-circle entirely appropriate to its

theme. There are, in fact, far fewer traces of inept craftsmanship in the play than in *Epitaph*, in spite of its occasional
expository lapses—as here, during Alison's over-explicit
recollection of her marriage:

> ALISON: It was just before the General Election, I remem-
> ber, and Nigel was busy getting himself into Parliament.
> He didn't have time for anyone but his constituents. Oh,
> he'd have been sweet and kind, I know.
> HELENA: Darling, why didn't you come to me?
> ALISON: You were away on tour in some play, I think.
> HELENA: So I was.
> ALISON: Those next few months at the flat in Poplar were a
> nightmare. . . . [43]

This seems to anticipate a slow fade into flashback, to the
accompaniment of memory-making music: and the reinforced idiom gives itself away. The need to draw into the
action the mother of Jimmy's sometime closest friend strikes a
similarly contrived note:

> And there's Hugh's mum, of course. I'd almost forgotten
> her. She's been a good friend to us, if you like. She's even
> letting me buy the sweet-stall off her in my own time. She
> only bought it for us, anyway. She's so fond of you. I can
> never understand why you're so—distant with her. [34]

Note the abrupt transition from the simple recollection of the
first two sentences to the assertive exposition of the rest. But
Hugh's mum lives (and, during the course of the action,
dies) offstage, a proletarian substitute for the mother from
whom Jimmy felt himself estranged. And it is in the gen-
uineness of his response to her death that she comes at last to
life, as more than a figment of working-class wish-fulfilment.

Another offstage character, and perhaps (or so Cliff suggests) another mother-substitute, [71] is Jimmy's first mistress, Madeline. She too comes in for clumsy handling, though the weakness here is in the rhetoric rather than the reportage:

> Her curiosity about things, and about people was staggering. It wasn't just a naïve nosiness. With her, it was simply the delight of being awake, and watching. [19]

This rings as false on stage as it does to the ear—partly because its careful, consecutive development reflects over-anxiety on Osborne's part to make his point, rather than Jimmy's usual, free-flowing stream-of-consciousness. Nor has Osborne quite lost the habit of apologising for an obtrusive dramatic convenience: thus, of Alison's confessional with Cliff in the first act, which serves a useful expository purpose, her confidant is made to mouth the fatal catch-phrase, "I've never heard you talking like this about him"! [30] Alison's retrospection for Helena's and the audience's benefit in the second act is another sequence during which the play's construction clumsily breaks surface. And if Josie's pregnancy in *Epitaph for George Dillon* had been over-timely, so is the mortality of Alison's infant in *Look Back in Anger*. A squalling child in Jimmy's attic, and things really would have to change: a miscarriage, and the bears and squirrels become even more vital as a means of making the old existence endurable.

In other respects, *Look Back in Anger* adapts the familiar mechanics of the naturalistic problem play comfortably enough. A first-act exposition culminates in the arrival of an outsider to develop the situation, as Helena duly develops it in act two, and the final act restores a kind of precarious *status quo*. Osborne has considerably more confidence now in

his curtains, which are—with one notable exception—
logical rather than cliffhanging culminations. The exception
is Helena's instant-seduction of Jimmy at the end of act two,
in the immediate aftermath of Alison's departure: [73-4] and
her equally sudden renunciation, which brings Jimmy and
Alison together again near the close of the play, [93] is no
more satisfactory. The indisputably dramatic quality of both
twists lends them theatrical viability, but it is a viability in a
vacuum.

Part of the trouble is that both Cliff and Helena function
rather as chemical agents than as characters. Cliff even
describes himself as a "no-man's land" between Alison and
Jimmy:

> This has always been a battlefield, but I'm pretty certain
> that if I hadn't been here, everything would have been
> over between these two long ago. I've been a—a no-man's
> land between them. Sometimes, it's been still and peaceful,
> no incidents, and we've all been reasonably happy. But
> most of the time, it's simply a very narrow strip of plain
> hell. But where I come from, we're used to brawling and
> excitement. Perhaps I even enjoy being in the thick of it. I
> love these two people very much. And I pity all of us. [60]

As the self-consistent idiom here suggests, Cliff is a much
more credible person than Helena, and he does instil both
stability and a sense of pity into the play, without which
Jimmy's astringency might fall victim to a law of diminishing
returns. The very incongruity of Cliff's friendship with
Jimmy makes it, in a sense, more acceptable. But Helena is
an altogether too-perfect embodiment of everything Jimmy
despises. The affair between them is necessary to the formal
shape of the play: but their mutual attraction is given very
little dramatic substance. To talk about an attraction of

opposites is only to give a name to the cliché that is being employed: and Osborne's quasi-psychological clues—the passionate clinch following the moment of violence, the shared sado-masochism of a sexual encounter between social enemies—are too neat to be true. Helena's seduction of Jimmy would seem trite even if she were adequately conceived as the upright anglican she proclaims herself—a reversion to which role is the lame excuse for her final departure. As it is, her whole existence seems little more than a dramatic convenience.

Perhaps it's worth remembering that in *Epitaph* there is a moment of casually motivated passion between George and Ruth similar to that which occurs between Jimmy and Helena. George's kiss leads to the long conversation at the core of the play. But Helena's leads straight to bed, and to a third act "several months later" [75] in which the growth of the resultant relationship can be taken for granted—just as the gradual blossoming of George and Josie's relationship in *Epitaph* had to be *assumed* at the same stage of the action. In terms of their patterning of emotional events, in fact, Osborne's two earliest plays develop with a marked similarity. Both have intervals at opportune moments, saving a lot of work in routine character-fulfilment: and Ruth's departure occurs at the same moment before the close of *Epitaph* as does Helena's at the end of *Look Back in Anger*. Both leave-takings are in part symbolic, and both are followed by just enough of an anti-climax before the final curtain to suggest the nature of the dramatic resolution.

Helena, however is no such potential soul-mate to Jimmy as Ruth was to George—but it does appear that Jimmy is reconciling himself to the same kind of animal relationship with Alison as George was contemplating with Josie. Isn't Alison in her squirrel's drey precisely that "warm, generous, honest-to-goodness animal lying at your side every night", which George sought as a "kind of euthanasia?" But the conclusion to *Epitaph* is conceived as a kind of defeat, and the conclusion to *Look Back in Anger* as a kind of triumph: for Jimmy and Alison achieve a self-realisation that George and Josie are never likely to share. Hence the climactic game of bears-and-squirrels—an animal relationship indeed. [96] So where *does* the difference between George and Jimmy begin? It begins, surely, along the line that divides the characters from their creator: the divide between generalising and particularising minds. To George and Jimmy, there are no special cases: each is a creature of sweeping condemnations and of fixed allegiances. But to Osborne every case is a special case: and Jimmy Porter's is a very special case indeed.

Jimmy, in his wife's words, has never known "what it was to feel young, really young". [28] Emotionally, he later suggests, he was old at the age of ten. Watching his father's slow death, he "learnt at an early age what it was to be angry—angry and helpless". He tells Helena:

> I knew more about—love . . . betrayal . . . and death, when I was ten years old than you will probably ever know all your life. [58]

Now none of this is necessarily *true:* but it is the persona Jimmy projects, and which has become inseparable— certainly inseparable on stage—from whatever kernel of unarticulated self remains beneath his protective shell of verbiage. Thus Jimmy has remained rooted in the past—a past of his own reshaping, created in the process of self-rationalisation. John Beavan, in an early review of the play,[11] complained that Jimmy's chosen lot was that of a thirties-intellectual going slumming rather than that of a disen-chanted socialist in the early fifties. But this is just the point. Only the *mythical* Jimmy Porter, the journalist's angry young man, is of the fifties. In reality, Jimmy's slumming takes the form of running a sweet-stall and choosing to live in much more squalid surroundings than the economics of any confectioner cashing-in on the abolition of sweet-rationing could possibly dictate. He chooses his squalor existentially: he is created and identified by it. He is not a *representative* character at all, still less morally detestable or exemplary: he has been shaped by personal circumstances which have left him self-consciously proletarian and sexually uncertain.

In fact, Jimmy's ethical system is so entirely a product of sentimentalised working-class puritanism that, for all his veneer of forthright sophistication, he is almost Victorian in his insistence upon keeping a sexual relationship in its proper place—in bed. Outside bed, brawling is "the only thing left I'm any good at". [53] Jimmy doesn't *talk* to his wife, except in anger or in allegory: and this is not really because he's "too much of a pig", as Cliff suggests, but because he's too much of a puritan to pay her any sexual compliment other than copulation. [31] His own hyper-gamous marriage has apparently damned him in the eyes of his former friends: and he is no doubt well aware that his wife's social condescension resembles that of his own mother —bourgeois intellectual as she was, "all for being associated with minorities, provided they were the smart, fashionable ones". [57]

To redeem that maternal guilt, Jimmy has sought a working-class mother-substitute in Hugh's mum, over whom he tear-jerks unashamedly. Thus, of his marriage to Alison he recalls

the first time I showed her your photograph—just after we were married. She looked at it, and the tears just welled up in her eyes, and she said: "But she's so beautiful! She's so beautiful!" She kept repeating it as if she couldn't

believe it. Sounds a bit simple and sentimental when you
repeat it. But it was pure gold the way she said it. [62]

This is no longer Osborne forestalling criticism of a possible
lapse in emotional taste. The lapse is Jimmy's, who really
does believe that the "simple and sentimental" is purified
by its proletarian source. His own verbal introversion
leads him into a curt defence of his words, for he would
otherwise be the first to condemn such self-indulgence as is
here transmuted into gold: he demands, in short, that
others recognise his own exceptions to his own rules.

Cliff is another exception: he is permitted, to Helena's
mystification, to be quite actively fond of Alison, who admits:

> It isn't easy to explain. It's what he would call a question
> of allegiances, and he expects you to be pretty literal about
> them. Not only about himself and all the things he
> believes in, his present and his future, but his past as well.
> All the people he admires and loves, and has loved. The
> friends he used to know, people I've never even known—
> and probably wouldn't have liked. His father, who died
> years ago. Even the other women he's loved. Do you
> understand? [42]

A demand for allegiance to his own past: if one *is* to understand Jimmy—and therefore the play—this is something that
has to be appreciated and accepted. Because Alison loves and
consequently needs Jimmy, and is prepared for co-existence
on almost any terms, she tries to offer the allegiance he
requires. Verbally, she is therefore made to stumble across an
endless assault-course—relieved only by occasional oases of
bears-and-squirrels fantasy. Osborne chooses such an oasis
as his climax, but only a few lines earlier Alison has been
"grovelling", [95] and there can be little doubt that she will

grovel again. For the bears-and-squirrels are inextricably woven into the "texture of ordinary despair" that is the fabric of the play.

Perhaps this was what a *Times Literary Supplement* leader was misunderstanding when it pontificated at the time of *Look Back in Anger*'s first production as follows:

> His maladjusted characters only really exist in the vortex of emotional vindictiveness which the writer creates with such uncomfortable vividness. All the externals of the misalliance, including the famous sweet-stall which the young man operates for his livelihood, do not seem quite integral.[12]

Of course the sweet-stall is not integral: it is part of a complex process of self-identification with a lost, proletarian innocence, as alien to the actual, university-educated Jimmy as the Spanish Civil War. And it is surely in this conflict between actual alienation and "applied" identification that *Look Back in Anger* did strike a chord in many radical breasts of the mid-fifties. What is *typical* about the play is its hero's consciousness of the conflict: what is eccentric is his attempt to reconcile it by means of a sort of enacted nostalgia. And his foredoomed failure to find fulfilment in such an attempt is at the root of his malaise. Jimmy's scorn, and his apparently unmotivated outbreaks of anger, derive from this failure, and in turn nourish it. He is caught in a vicious circle: and in this sense the play's return to what is effectively a *status quo* is both formally and thematically appropriate.

Look Back in Anger, then, seems to me to be basically a well-made problem play of considerable psychological insight. I hope I have not over-psychologised it: if I have, it is in an attempt to correct the usual tendency to over-socialise it. But what must one really make of the "little ordinary human enthusiasm" and the "good, brave causes" for which Jimmy says he longs, and from which have been woven so much of the subsequent mythology? It may help to recall the actual contexts of these over-familiar quotations. Jimmy's desire for "ordinary human enthusiasm" [15] is an ironical plea for interest in an article in one of the posh newspapers: and his comment on the absence of good causes is an after-thought to an assertion that he is being bled to death by all the women in the world, not to mention the postmaster-general. [84–5] The irony, in context, inevitably modifies the response: but this is not to suggest that the emotional *need* for brave causes, expressed out of context, wasn't entirely characteristic of a prevailing mood in the year of the Suez War and the Hungarian Revolution.

Look Back in Anger therefore became, in spite of itself, a harbinger of the New Left, of Anti-Apartheid, and of the Campaign for Nuclear Disarmament. But I don't think Jimmy Porter would have been clamouring for his member-ship cards: his emotional needs may have been typical, but his response to them was exceptional—a word Osborne has himself used to describe the condition of his heroes. At once more sensitive and more skewed than George Dillon, Jimmy Porter could have found no more permanent an identity on a protest march than in the warm, animal comfort of his squirrel's drey: and given a few more years, he might well have found himself reduced to the refuges of an Archie Rice —to gin, to a succession of casual mistresses, and to looking back in increasingly hopeless nostalgia over the years that divided him from his instinctive heritage.

3

The Entertainer

OUTBURSTS OF CLOWNING at once brighten and slightly scorch the polished surface-actions of *Epitaph for George Dillon* and *Look Back in Anger*. For these actions are naturalistic: and their comic interludes, in spite of stabs at motivation, thus constitute more or less self-conscious set-pieces. Such is the impression, at least, left by George Dillon's patter as he "plays" the cocktail cabinet, or by Jimmy and Cliff's duologue between T. S. Eliot and Pam—which even breaks into supposedly spontaneous song. But George Dillon was, after all, a failed actor by profession, and Jimmy Porter an instinctive one, accustomed to merging his real, vulnerable self into the familiar persona of the contemptuous cynic. And now, in *The Entertainer* the outer as well as the inner world of Osborne's characters is theatrical. So, accordingly, is the shape of his play: its acts and scenes are laid out like a variety programme, and Archie Rice's short "turns"—ostensibly the comic leavening to a strip-show—are sandwiched between the longer "sketches" involving the rest of his family.

This is not so revolutionary a development in Osborne's formal technique as at first it seems. There are still three acts, within which the lengthier "sketches" are written realistically, as if for a fixed domestic-interior: and despite its lack of scenic definition, this is effectively how the Rice's living-room functions. Thus, the play's stylisation is largely a matter of externals—though Osborne's opening stage-direction foreshadows a much more organic process of vulgarising its action:

The lighting is the kind you expect to see in the local Empire—everything bang-on, bright and hard, or a simple follow-spot. The scenes and interludes must, in fact, be lit as if they were simply turns on the bill. Furniture and props are as basic as they would be for a short sketch. On both sides of the proscenium is a square in which numbers —the turn numbers—appear. The problems involved are basically the same as those that confront any resident stage-manager on the twice nightly circuit every Monday morning of his working-life. [12]

Now merely to subject a prestige-production, to which England's greatest living actor is lending his services, to shoestring stage-management does not in itself guarantee a scruffy music-hall atmosphere. How, it has to be asked, do the domestic scenes stand up *functionally* to being mounted, turn-numbers and all, as run-of-the-mill music-hall sketches? And in what ways do the intervening "turns" counterpoint the sketches? Are they purposefully related to them—or are the styles no more than arbitrarily dissonant?

Here, first, is Osborne's explanatory note on the subject:

The music hall is dying, and, with it, a significant part of England. Some of the heart of England has gone; something that once belonged to everyone, for this was truly a folk art. In writing this play, I have not used some of the techniques of the music hall in order to exploit an effective trick, but because I believe that these can solve some of the eternal problems of time and space that face the dramatist and, also, it has been relevant to the story and setting. Not only has this technique its own traditions, its own convention and symbol, its own mystique, it cuts right across the restrictions of the so-called naturalistic stage. Its contact is immediate, vital, and direct. [7]

In fact, most of the family episodes, given orthodox visual trimmings, would fit quite snugly onto a "so-called naturalistic stage". They add up into a problem play, about an unfaithful and unsuccessful husband and his fragmented family, who are confronted with the technically expedient crisis of the violent death of one of their sons, the innocent victim of terrorist retaliation in Cyprus. And in these episodes, orthodox in form albeit challenging in theme, such technical problems as are evidently better solved than in *Look Back in Anger* nevertheless derive from Osborne's dependence upon similar conventions.

Exposition, for example, is even less obtrusive. In fact the opening dialogue between Billy Rice and Jean—a grandfather with a tendency to reminisce, and a granddaughter long absent from home—gets most of it across very neatly. And the later retrospection is psychologically as well as dramatically necessary: for in a sense all the elder members of the Rice family are living in their own separate pasts, and their indulgence in nostalgia is compulsive. Phoebe, Archie's long-suffering wife, is anecdotal almost to the point of senility —the aggressive senility of the self-pitying, from which Archie has been suffering time out of mind:

PHOEBE: You don't understand—
ARCHIE: I know. Phoebe scrubbed a dining hall floor for five hundred kids when she was twelve years old, didn't you?
PHOEBE: Oh—
ARCHIE: Didn't you? Have you any idea, any of you, have you any idea how often she's told me about those five hundred kids and that dining hall? [54]

But one's very sense of Phoebe's self-absorption gives dramatic point to her rambling recollections, which fulfil an incidental purpose as background narrative—as, for example does her retrospective tale of Brother Bill's loaded generosity in the sixth number. [49–51]

Not only does the play achieve temporal depth by such means, but social context as well. The feeling of a particular *locale* is, in fact, stronger than in either *Epitaph* or *Look Back in Anger*: for one cannot readily imagine George Dillon during his desultory quests for work beyond the Elliots' drawing-room, or Jimmy Porter—in spite of the film—haggling at his sweet-stall. But one can very easily picture Archie Rice drinking beyond his means at the Rockliffe—"that damned place down by the clock tower", as Billy describes it [17]— or his father in the saloon bar of the humbler but gaudily modernised Cambridge. It is, then, worth considering how the play succeeds at such a naturalistic level—because it *does* succeed—before broaching the stylistic problems raised by Osborne's intended imposition of music-hall style.

Osborne's earlier plays drew upon the time-honoured convention of consecutive speech—that is, the assumption that characters either listen to other characters, and reply appropriately, or purposely refrain from so doing. The verbalised stream-of-consciousness is both logical and shared. *The Entertainer* works from no such rational premise: it more nearly assumes that *nobody* listens to anyone else. Of Phoebe, it's aptly alleged that she is "never still, she never listens— like most of the people in this house", [25] and later both Jean and Billy—independently, but within a few lines of one other—comment on the same phenomenon. [78] Osborne handles the resultant *non-sequiturs*, which follow up the separate preoccupations of his characters, with a sure feeling for the shading-off processes between thought and speech, and this is symptomatic of the fullness he has at last achieved in his characterisation. Indeed, this and the much later

Hotel in Amsterdam remain the most fully *reciprocal* plays Osborne has written.

Frank's bantering "relationship substitute" [51] with his father, Phoebe's interminable incarceration in her own past, and Archie's sense of just how far he dare go in provoking his father—all have the warp and woof of the complex, loving and hating fabric of family. Even Archie's recurrent objection to the absence of draught Bass in Toronto suggests the kind of in-joke most families share: and Phoebe's sudden, last-straw fury with Billy, when he anticipates the cutting of the cake intended to celebrate Mick's return, is a textbook example of conflict that is almost unmotivated, yet assured in its feeling for the raw edges of domesticity. [56–7]

There was some sense of this kind of slowly maturing interdependence between members of a family in the relationship between Alison and her father in *Look Back*: and it contrasted strangely in that play with one's impression that Alison and Jimmy knew each other if anything rather less well than when they first met. But many of Osborne's earlier characters were apt to indulge in instant-relationships, usually of a sexual kind—and *The Entertainer* is not entirely free from this blemish. For George and Josie, Jimmy and Helena, and now for Jean and her background boyfriend Graham Dodd, sex is a matter of a "given" physical attraction, not one element in a relationship that *can't help* developing in other directions. How Jimmy Porter occupied himself for "several months" with Helena during the second interval of *Look Back in Anger*, or what George and Josie said to each other outside the dance-hall or the double-bed, is hard enough to imagine: and it is equally difficult to understand how Jean and Graham in *The Entertainer* know so little of each other. Jean is not unaware of this:

You know, I hadn't realised—it just hadn't occurred to me

that you could love somebody, that you could want them, and want them twenty-four hours of the day and then suddenly find that you're neither of you even living in the same world. I don't understand that. I just don't understand it. I wish I could understand it. It's frightening. Sorry, Phoebe, I shouldn't be drinking your gin. . . . [29]

The point here is not that such temperamental incompatibility is infrequent or even improbable—for, as Jimmy Porter and Alison have discovered, there are ways of transcending it. It is rather that Jean, as Osborne conceives her, is the last person to perpetuate a relationship on a purely physical level—and that Graham, when he eventually appears on the scene, is still less likely to have invented a bears-and-squirrels method of sublimating the couple's differences.

Conversely, Archie and Phoebe—not unlike Mrs Elliot and Percy in *George Dillon*—maintain a sort of temperamental truce, but cross no physical boundaries towards one another. It is not necessarily an adverse criticism of the *depth* of Osborne's conception of such lop-sided relationships to assert this point: but it is a reflection on the *range* of his powers as a dramatist that he was and, until *Hotel in Amsterdam*, remained unwilling to portray—even by way of background contrast—a moderately full (not necessarily successful) relationship between a normally sexed couple.

As for Graham Dodd, he makes all the expected noises. Osborne's comment is revealing:

There are plenty of these around—well dressed, assured, well educated, their emotional and imaginative capacity so limited it is practically negligible. They have an all-defying inability to associate themselves with anyone in circumstances even slightly dissimilar to their own.

Graham Dodd doesn't need much description. If you can't recognise him, it's for one reason only. [83]

But there is a failure of sympathy—or, to be pedantic, of empathy—on Osborne's part also. He is too blinded by revulsion to associate *himself* with anyone in circumstances even remotely similar to Graham Dodd's. Of course there are plenty of dramatists who populate play after play exclusively with Dodd and his kind: and Osborne's failure to portray the man as more than a self-caricature would matter little in itself, but for the necessity to convince an audience that once upon a time Jean Rice thought she loved such a person.

Brother Bill, who turns up with a final offer to tide Archie over his latest economic crisis, on condition that he emigrates to Canada, [84–5] is more or less identical with Graham Dodd—as Osborne's admission that the latter "may well be like him in thirty years" [83] confirms. The point is perhaps worth generalising: in Osborne's plays there are on the one hand interesting and "exceptional" people and on the other the unfortunate rest. In *The Entertainer*, Billy Rice falls into the "interesting" category, of those who are wrong but sympathetic, and his son into the "exceptional" grouping— of those who are wrong and unsympathetic to boot, but who are redeemed by their nonconformity.

The Entertainer is polarised along such an axis between Archie and Billy: but these two are the *only* characters who fit into the play at each of its levels. The other members of the family—Phoebe, Jean and Frank—have to be discussed in quasi-psychological terms because they are conceived as individuals, and are interesting as individuals, within a naturalistic context of motivation and of plot-progression. But Billy and Archie are not only "realistic" characters: they are also embodiments of a dying way of life. The music-hall acts which break up the family episodes are almost exclusively

Archie's, and it is he alone who bridges the stylistic gulf between the play's "sketches" and its intervening "turns". Thus, the reason for Frank's appearance in the number-nine spot on the bill is obscure: the previous scene has ended in Archie's blues lament for the murdered Mick, [73] and Frank's follow-up number [74] is remarkable only for its uniquely unironical tone.

> Those playing fields of Eton
> Have really got us beaten,

he sings: and the sentiment is no more apposite than the rhyme.

Archie's blues close the second act—again, the strong curtain proving an irresistible temptation, though in lesser hands than Olivier's these are excruciatingly difficult moments to handle—and Frank's song opens the third, which quickly moves into the post-funeral sketch. Archie gets two solo-spots in this and in the first act, but only a single "turn" in the second. The earlier turns are entirely dissociated from the family scenes, and typically consist of brief and blue patter followed by "a little song I wrote myself". [24] These songs are rather peculiar combinations of jingoistic content and sentimental style: their unironic counterparts vanished with the last of the music halls. But the subject-matter is by no means random, and each of the three songs in acts one and two has its own particular target. "Why should I care" [24–5] eulogises apathy in the second turn, "We're all out for good old number one" [32–3] elevates chauvinism to a national virtue in the fourth, and "Now I'm just an ordinary bloke" [60–1] pushes the advantages of "normality", social and sexual, in the seventh. These numbers do have a cumulative force, picking off three of Osborne's pet hates with successive blows, and they foreshadow the style of the lyrics in *The World of Paul Slickey*, while working rather better in the distanced music-hall setting than their over-neatly contextualised successors in that play. But they fail to *connect* with the family episodes: they give local colour to Archie's career, but never relate his own failure to the national decadence they parody and proclaim.

In the final act, however, there is some attempt to blend the sketches and turns into a sort of surreal collage. The eleventh number [83] is an expository lead-in to Billy's funeral—indeed, its singular but successful use for such a purpose negatively emphasises the unnecessary orthodoxy of the earlier exposition. And in the final, thirteenth number, Archie is actually helped upstage by Phoebe—the income-tax man, a sort of updated Gyntian button-moulder, waiting in the wings with his hook—as he concludes a long rambling anecdote about the "little, ordinary man" who swore in heaven, to the infinite relief of the saint on entry duty. [87–8] The story has a certain pathos, and is perhaps microcosmic of Archie's vain struggle to stem the "progress" which is sweeping him away. But its relevance to the action is doubtful. Is this the dying fall of Archie's own career, or an appeal to all men of little or ordinary demeanour to blow verbal raspberries at respectability?

It certainly makes an odd contrast with the final family sketch, which ends by juxtaposing Jean and Graham down right with Archie and Brother Bill down left. Their conversations intersect:

JEAN: Here we are, we're alone in the universe, there's no God, it just seems that it all began by something as simple as sunlight striking on a piece of rock. And here we are. We've only got ourselves. Somehow, we've just got to make a go of it. *We've only ourselves.*

BROTHER BILL: I'm sorry Archie, but I've given up trying to understand. [85]

The staging and the dialogue alike emphasise the diametrical opposition between the values of Graham Dodd and Brother Bill, and those of Archie Rice and his daughter—whose unexpected closeness has been foreshadowed by successive, faltering attempts to talk to each other throughout the play. Ultimately, the attempts break down: and Archie's failure to communicate with his daughter derives from Jimmy Porter's disease—an inability to live in the present.

Now it is in this respect that both the formal shape and the temporal setting of *The Entertainer* begin to take on added significance. Not only can the play be fixed in time as the product of a particular decade, but as the product of a particular year. It is set in the aftermath of the Suez crisis: a time of demonstrations in Trafalgar Square, trouble in colonial Cyprus, and the impending resignation of a Prime Minister. To describe 1956 as a political watershed—to which the Hungarian revolution, the only one of these events not mentioned in the play, also contributed its undercurrents—is commonplace enough. And these elements in a world crisis were certainly among the forces which set the political reflexes of the young newly twitching: but they also hastened the death-rattle of the papery-tiger of British imperialism.

Not only the music-hall is dying in *The Entertainer*, therefore, but the way of life which gave it nourishment—on which Billy Rice's shabby-gentility sheds some rather faded light. In Osborne's own description of Billy there are echoes of the reluctant respect he accorded Colonel Redfern in *Look Back in Anger*:

Billy Rice is a spruce man in his seventies. He has great physical pride, the result of a life-time of being admired as

c

a "fine figure of a man". He is slim, upright, athletic. He glows with scrubbed well-being. His hair is just grey, thick and silky from its vigorous daily brush. His clothes are probably twenty-five years old—including his pointed patent leather shoes—but well-pressed and smart. His watch chain gleams, his collar is fixed with a tie-pin beneath the tightly knotted black tie, his brown homburg is worn at a very slight angle. When he speaks it is with a dignified Edwardian diction—a kind of repudiation of both Oxford and cockney that still rhymes "cross" with "force", and yet manages to avoid being exactly upper-class or effete. Indeed, it is not an accent of class but of period. One does not hear it often now. [13]

And there is something of the ambivalent regret of that final sentence in one of Billy's own remarks:

I feel sorry for you people. You don't know what it's really like. You haven't lived, most of you. You've never known what it was like, you're all miserable really. You don't know what life can be like. [23]

This is a curtain speech: but Billy is presented throughout the play as a man worthy of respect, who is usually accorded it. There is thus a strong element of wish-fulfilment in Archie's eventual attempt to stage a comeback for his father. In the family argument this generates, and in these lines of Jean's in particular, the attitudes of the three generations involved are markedly in contrast:

He's the only one of us who has any dignity or respect for himself, he's the only one of us who has anything at all, and you're going to murder him, you're going to take him down to—who is it—Rubens and Klein tomorrow morning at twelve-thirty, and you're going to let Mr Rubens and Mr Klein sign his death certificate. What are you letting yourself in for now, how on earth did you ever get him to do such a thing? What's happened to him? What's happened to his sense of self-preservation? [82]

A lot depends on the answer to this question, for an audience must sense, with Jean, that Billy is too self-aware to be an accomplice in the destruction of his dignity—and, in the event, of himself. Unfortunately, the flimsy excuse actually offered—that he "feels he owes it" to Archie for revealing to the parents of some saloon-bar tart that his son is a married man [82]—is one of the few moments of the play when probability is subordinated to plot-line.

But Billy's death is *symbolically* appropriate, because it marks the point at which Archie's struggle to hold back the historical process is finally rendered futile. As a human being rather than a symbol, Billy is really far better reconciled to the passing of his era, and of himself, than his son. "I keep telling him—it's dead already", [18] he says, of "the business" Archie is trying to perpetuate. And the "business" is only one aspect of an atrophying way of life to which Archie still clings. He is unable to confront the loneliness his daughter has perceived and accepted in the universe, and his life is spent in an evasive attempt to stitch up his own little corner of a disintegrating social fabric. It is, of course, doomed to fail. His parent finds comfort in resignation, his daughter in active rebellion: he alone is of a lost generation, caught at a turn of history's tide.

The importance of the music-hall acts lies, then, in their revelation of the "ideal" Archie Rice. "I have a go, don't I?" is his catch-phrase in the "little round world of light" in which we last see him. [88-9] And in the family-scenes,

Archie only communicates by adapting his stage persona to his domestic life—as Osborne specifies:

> Whatever he says to anyone is almost always very carefully "thrown away". Apparently absent minded, it is a comedian's technique, it absolves him from seeming committed to anyone or anything. [34]

His clichés "dropping like bats from the ceiling" [62] are thus as much part of the act as his dedication to draught Bass. And one feels that Osborne is much more objectively aware of Archie's shortcomings than he was of Jimmy Porter's, or even of George Dillon's. There is no special pleading. Archie's father does not die in agony, watched over by a boy being robbed of his childhood—but is effectively destroyed by his son in the very process of trying to perpetuate the past.

Archie is identified as much by the manner as the matter of his speech. At moments of stress he breaks into the jaggedly overlapping idiom of his stage-act:

> Did I ever tell you the greatest compliment I had paid to me—the greatest compliment I always treasure? I was walking along the front somewhere—I think it was here actually—one day, oh, it must be twenty-five years ago, I was quite a young man. Well, there I was walking along the front, to meet what I think we used to call a piece of crackling. Or perhaps it was a bit of fluff. No that was earlier. Anyway, I know I enjoyed it afterwards. But the point is I was walking along the front, all on my own, minding my own business . . . and two nuns came towards me—two nuns—[42]

And he finally trails off into the fall of the first-act curtain, the climax to his opening attempt to re-establish a rapport with his daughter. Phoebe's repetitiveness is different—a matter of reassuring rather than reasserting herself. And Billy, on the other hand, allows his words to follow his thoughts with an habitual care only slightly neglected in his senility—building up images in layers, then deflecting their sense if he has offended against his own code of propriety in the process. Thus, to Jean:

> Yes, you always used to like coming to see me, didn't you? You used to enjoy yourself with me when you were a little girl. You were a pretty little thing. With your dark curls and your little dresses. (*Quickly.*) Not that looks are everything. Not even for a woman. Don't you believe it. You don't look at the mantelpiece when you poke the fire. [23]

Archie would have toyed with that final image, extending it into a string of staccato sentences: for his use of language has the comedian's self-consciousness. It is a suit of protective armour to his father's old-fashioned frock-coat. In none of the earlier plays, in short, has Osborne so successfully differentiated between the linguistic habits of his characters.

It has been remarked that the Rices spend a considerable proportion of *The Entertainer*'s stage-time in various degrees of inebriation. Naturalistically, of course, this helps to effect a loosening of tongues—but it is a loosening of a distinctively alcoholic kind. The play contains a monstrous deal of sentiment, because sentiment is the verbal medium for nostalgia. But the corollary of an absorption in the past is an acute dread of the future: and the prevailing inebriation of the Rice family brings fears of mortality to the surface just as it encourages the nostalgic self-indulgence of the middle-generation. In addition to this concern for the past and the future, there *is* a fumbling towards the present in the play: and in the cases of Archie and Phoebe, this consists in their enforced confrontation with Mick's death. In the case of Billy it derives from a kind of self-recognition, and in that of Jean in her preoccupation with immediate political issues.

It is worth noting that Osborne selected one of the family scenes from *The Entertainer*—part of the sixth number—for a recent anthology of extracts from contemporary plays. His choice was determined by an understandable desire to demonstrate

> that my work does not consist entirely of dramatic monologues delivered by a central character striding a vague context inhabited by dramatic nonentities.[13]

But in concluding this preface to the extract, Osborne's reflection on the function of drama seems particularly relevant to his chosen play:

> Drama rests on the dynamic that is created between characters on the stage. It must be concrete and it must be expressed, even if it is only in silence or a gesture of despair. The theatre is not a school room, nor is it, as many people seem to think, a place where "discussion" takes place, where ideas are apparently formally examined in the manner of a solitary show-off in an intellectual magazine. It is a place where people spend much of their time responding nakedly—or failing—to the burden of trying to live and preparing to die.[14]

Admittedly, this is the kind of all-weather purpose it is possible to attribute to any serious play under the sun—including "intellectual" discussion plays—with some measure of truth: but *The Entertainer* does seem to demonstrate it in a rather precise way.

At the end of the long, self-flagellating diatribe with which Osborne's extract opens, Archie turns from his own failings to those of his wife:

> Look at her. What has she got to do with people like you? People of intellect and sophistication. She's very drunk, and just now her muzzy, under-developed, untrained mind is racing because her blood stream is full of alcohol I can't afford to give her, and she's going to force us to listen to all sorts of dreary embarrassing things we've all heard a hundred times before. She's getting old, and she's worried about who's going to keep her when she can't work any longer. She's afraid of ending up in a long box in somebody else's front room in Gateshead, or was it West Hartlepool?
> [54–5]

The manner in which exposition derives in *The Entertainer* from a *compulsive* picking-over of past events has already been mentioned—and sure enough, Archie is here taking up an allusion of Phoebe's in the previous scene:

> I don't want to always have to work. I mean you want a bit of life before it's all over. It takes all the gilt off if you know you've got to go on and on till they carry you out in a box. It's all right for him, he's all right. He's still got his women. While it lasts anyway. But I don't want to end up being laid out by some stranger in some rotten stinking little street in Gateshead, or West Hartlepool or another of those dead-or-alive holes! [40]

All the elderly or middle-aged Rices are "preparing to die". Billy achieves his death, robbed of the dignity with which he might have confronted it. Phoebe ponders on being laid out in strange lodgings. And Archie celebrates another year in which the income-tax man has been successfully evaded in the wings.

Paradoxically, however, the *actual* deaths of Billy and of the unseen Mick fail to make more than an incidental impression: and the scene after Mick's funeral is characterised by retrospection rather than grief. It also provokes Archie into stating, half-seriously and half-ironically, his own object in life:

> Shall I tell you—all my life I've been searching for something. I've been searching for a draught Bass you can drink all the evening without running off every ten minutes, that you can get drunk on without feeling sick, and all for fourpence. Now, the man who could offer me all of that would really get my vote. He really would. [76]

But a few exchanges later, Archie himself qualifies the symbolic significance of his draught Bass motif:

> Listen, kiddie, you're going to find out that in the end nobody really gives a damn about anything except some little animal something. And for me that little animal something is draught Bass. [76]

Of course, Archie is not quite as "dead behind the eyes" as he has earlier declared himself. [72] It's important to remember Osborne's own warning against taking Archie at his word[15] —either in his declared incapacity for feeling, or in his advice to Jean to deaden her own responses:

> I think you really feel something . . . in spite of all that

Trafalgar Square stuff. You're what they call a senti-
mentalist. You carry all your responses about with you,
instead of leaving them at home. . . . [71]

It has to be noted, before questioning whether Archie really
has lost the ability to feel, that this speech is set in close
proximity to his famous reverie about the "old fat negress
getting up to sing about Jesus or something".

I've never heard anything like that since. I've never heard
it here. . . . Oh, he's heard it. Billy's heard it. He's heard
them singing. Years ago, poor old gubbins. But you won't
hear it anywhere now. I don't suppose we'll ever hear it
again. There's nobody who can feel like that. [70-1]

The emotional self-indulgence of this romanticising of a
bar-singer is surely not Osborne's, as some critics have
charged. It is quite characteristically Archie's. Osborne
himself is well aware of the dangers of living in the past or
despairing of the present, as he is of the kinds of dissociation
it induces. He has defined the sexual form of this dissociation
in the cleavage between Jimmy Porter and Alison. Here, he
generalises its effects, and simultaneously justifies his choice
of a music-hall form. For Archie's "little world of light"—
the world of negro bar-singers and of music-hall troupers—
finally merges into his real life, and the light "snaps out". [89]
    Jean's earlier conversation with Graham has pointed such
bleak hope as remains: but because Jean is basically a well-
adjusted person, Osborne shows little interest in her, except
in so far as she can act as a catalyst to the more estranged
characters. With how her political beliefs might effect or
nourish her own life, let alone those of others, Osborne is not
concerned—any more than he is concerned with Constance's
parliamentary life in *Time Present*. The brave causes have

simply been roll-called and espoused, offering to Jean's younger generation some hope of a reactive sanity.

But Archie Rice—who resembles Bill Maitland, in *Inadmissible Evidence*, more than any other Osborne hero—has rejected even this substitute for reciprocity in his relationships. He is, in short, exceptional—in the sense that Osborne in an *Observer* article, published just before the first production of *The Entertainer* in April 1957, had suggested that all theatrically viable characters should be. After an attack on the "adjustment" school of criticism ("Why doesn't he stop loafing about and try a good job of work?" "Why doesn't she face up to her responsibilities and snap out of it?"), Osborne went on to talk about Tennessee Williams's *Streetcar Named Desire*:

> The argument of the adjustment school is that characters like Blanche and Brick are not "normal", and they aren't like *us*. In fact, they are, yes—neurotics. Now this attitude is, I believe, built on a complete misconception of what theatre—or, indeed, art—is about. Adler said somewhere that the neurotic is like the normal individual only more so. A neurotic is not less adequate than an auditorium full of "normals". Every character trait is a neurosis writ small. I like my plays writ large, and that is how these are written.[16]

Now the Rices, as Archie says, have "problems that nobody's ever heard of", because they are "so remote from the rest of ordinary everyday, human experience." [54] And Archie himself suggests, albeit ironically, a cold-bath treatment for their problems:

> Come on love, pull yourself together. That's what we should have done years ago. Pulled ourselves together. Let's pull ourselves together. (*Sings.*) Let's pull ourselves

together, together, together. Let's pull ourselves together, and the happier we'll be! [58]

This is Archie in his best, bludgeoning mood, moulding, as so often in the dialogue of *The Entertainer*, the repetitive rhythms of music-hall patter—each phrase tripping over and into the next—into a verbal truncheon with which to clobber the "adjustment school". For Osborne's interest as a dramatist has always been in the sort of "neurotic" people to whose problems and personalities the school's simplified solutions are irrelevant.

Far from being the apostle of the commonplace or the kitchen-sink, therefore, Osborne has instead been concerned to expand human awareness by portraying exceptional and, more often than not, unsympathetic characters, in a manner which forces them upon the attention of an auditorium full of "normals". That such sympathies at times cut him off *too* completely from the unexceptional may be a human failing, but dramatically it is a limitation within which he has usually been able to work. With *The Entertainer*, however, Osborne had written himself out, for a while, on the theme of *looking back*, and he evidently wished to attempt something in a lighter vein, directly though critically related to the "ordinary" irritations of life which were increasingly impinging on his personal privacy. The result was that unwise adventure outside his chosen boundaries, into *The World of Paul Slickey*.

4

The World of Paul Slickey

JOHN OSBORNE must have experienced something approaching catharsis after the first night of his first musical—which now seems likely to remain his last. Its own and its audience's excesses of fury and contempt must surely have combined to effect a kind of purgation—and in this sense *Slickey* might reasonably be regarded as a play Osborne *had* to write. But granted his desire to give *theatrical* expression to the attack on the establishment launched in his *Declaration* credo,[17] why did he pick on the ultra-establishment vehicle of musical-comedy in which to continue it? *The Entertainer* had, of course, helped to wean him away from naturalism: and it had also permitted him to express ideas illustrative of his main action—though strictly speaking extraneous to it—by means of set-piece songs. But such a hybrid form had built-in limitations, however appropriately it fitted *The Entertainer*'s music-hall theme: at least, it was scarcely adaptable to a dramatised hatepiece directed against the press and the peerage. In *Slickey*, therefore, these twin targets were loosely linked by the gossip-columnist hero's convoluted implication in a set of stately-home adulteries: and musical-comedy may well have seemed the most malleable means of combining such a farcically-oriented plot, which reflected only certain of the attitudes Osborne was concerned to expose, with more tangentially-directed songs.

And yet how much more stimulating *Slickey* would have been if its musical-comedy form had been chosen in order to betray the expectations it aroused—that is, if Osborne, instead of merely *using* the form, had roundly abused it, along with all the establishmentarians who peopled his plot. In fact, he took his medium so seriously as to open the musical at the Pavilion Theatre, Bournemouth, and to transfer it, in May 1959, to the Palace Theatre in the heart of London's West End, where not so long afterwards it was succeeded by *The Sound of Music*. Now a burlesque musical would have been ideally suited to Osborne's satirical purposes—but his attempt to realise these theatrically in the straightforward songs and dances of *The World of Paul Slickey* met with consequences akin to decanting vinegar into a cask of mild ale. Osborne set his satiric songs to an unexceptionable score—and merely emphasised its unsuitability for his purposes. The result, as *Encore* put it at the time was "impudent, satirical, profane, revolutionary, unique and bad".[18]

The plot of *Paul Slickey* lands its eponymous hero in the stately-home of his father-in-law, Lord Mortlake. He holds a journalistic watching-brief of which the family is ignorant: for Mortlake, though at death's door, is within hours of evading estate-duties, by chalking up the statutory five years after the premature disposal of his worldly goods. His final hours are thus the cliffhanging-edge along which the plot teeters. Slickey himself—otherwise Jack Oakham—is in love with his sister-in-law Deirdre. He ends up alongside her in the laboratory of mad Uncle George, who has discovered an elixir for instant changes of sex. The illicit relationship of Slickey's wife Lesley, a brassière tycoon, and Deirdre's parliamentarian husband Michael completes the play's pattern of mutual adulteries. Also caught up in its complications, however, are a prospective debutante named Gillian— who falls in love with a pop-singer called Terry Maroon—her mother Mrs Giltedge-Whyte, and the ethereal Lady Mortlake. Both these elderly ladies have been enamoured of his dying lordship in their pasts, generating Deirdre, Lesley and—it is eventually revealed—Gillian in the process.

The slightest of realignments, and this jigsaw-puzzle of pairings might have become incestuous—an added convolution the last-minute affair between Deirdre and a sexually metamorphosed Lesley actually achieves. But if *Slickey* was indeed intended to further an incidental gospel of sexual tolerance, such as *Under Plain Cover* later espoused, the intention remains as much on the play's periphery as do the journalistic goings-on of Paul Slickey himself. And this suggests the flaw in the play's plotting which complicates, as it were, its formal weakness: it starts all kinds of thematic balls rolling, but lets each in turn trickle out of sight instead of choosing one or two to slam into purposeful goals.

The World of Paul Slickey is prefaced by a sort of anti-dedication, a vituperative attack on the breed of corrupt journalists it set out to satirise—"those who handle their professions as instruments of debasement". [5] But this appendage was presumably written in the wake of the play's disastrous reception: for Slickey himself is, on the whole, the least objectionable of Osborne's gallery of petty rogues. He has even, it appears, turned down an offer of alternative employment as dramatic critic, on the grounds that he takes the theatre too seriously—and he incidentally appears to share with his creator an exaggerated idea of the monetary rewards of reviewing. He has even been trying to write a play. But he has been misled into the kind of diverted outlet for his literary talents in which, but for the grace of Josie, George Dillon might have found himself engaged:

Jack has always suffered from excessive aspiration. There is a constant stain of endeavour underneath his emotional armpits. It throws off quite an unpleasant smell of sour ideals. [50]

Lesley's vignette of her husband might sum up any of the early Osborne heroes. And an early Osborne hero is very much what Jack becomes, granted the distorting-effect of the conventions within which he has to take shape.

Thus, it's not hard to envisage Jimmy Porter's anger deteriorating into Slickey's readiness to manipulate the "moronic public taste": [15] but there is one essential difference. Osborne never really conceives Jack as more than a character conforming to the dramatic need of a particular moment. When a mouthpiece for an onslaught against the arbitrarily introduced pop-singer is required, Jack's the boy:

Do you hear that nasal blubbering about little flowers and watching new-born babies cry? Of loving you, and no one but you? Baby, you're all mine, all mine through all eternity? That so-called man in there is making two thousand pounds a week . . . for what? For emptying the slop buckets of modern love into a microphone, for crawling and cringing before the almighty tyranny of the bosom. [75]

The muddled but forceful scatology of that last sentence could well be Jimmy Porter's: but back at his gossip-columnist's desk, Jack declares himself incapable of such redeeming passion. And the stylistic context is such that extenuating pleas about a lack of self-knowledge lose all relevance, for it is a representative role that he here fulfils:

And practically everybody, anybody, anything
You can think of leaves me
Quite, completely
Newspaper neatly
Quite, quite cold. [14]

The quality of the lyric is representative: and its contradiction is crucial. Passion is always a redeeming feature of Osborne's heroes: but Oakham can scarcely be taken very seriously as a hero, for *his* redeeming passion is only an intermittent and functional dilution of his gutter-press vulgarity.

It first appears, as the play opens and as its title promises, that *The World of Paul Slickey* is to be a send-up of the methods and morals of gossip-columnists, as exemplified in the practises of Slickey himself. His newspaper, dominated as it is by an elderly, titled proprietor, more or less resembles the *Daily Express*—though the journal is actually dubbed, conforming to Osborne's taste for comic-strip nomenclature, the *Daily Racket*. And the first scene of the play seems to state its satirical premise:

A shoddy little talent and a sawn-off imagination
Will never be allowed to go to waste,
While *we* have got our ear-holes to the heart-beat of the
        nation,
And our great big working finger on the moronic public
        taste. [15]

Here the "public taste" is represented sympathetically—by implication—as the object of journalistic manipulation. But a few lines later the range of attack is extended, as the chorus of journalists recites an ironic catechism of common-man common-sense:

Come off it you intellectuals!
British common-sense will always prevail!
What on earth are they angry about!
We are the majority, we are the ones who matter!

Most people are jolly hopeful, thank goodness!
I believe in Britain!
Life is quite morbid enough as it is!
We are solid and so are you. [16]

At this point Jack Oakham chips in with "Remember our brave fighting ships," and Osborne is tempted into a brief, interpolated burlesque of public-school naval heroics. [16–17] This is passably amusing of its kind: and at this point it seems quite appropriate to the kaleidoscopic impression the play is beginning to make.

Already, Jack and his secretary-cum-mistress have been called upon to attempt some complicated transitions between the colloquial and the camp, though whether the exposition in the following exchanges is intended as self-parody is not entirely clear:

JO: You mean to say that your wife's family don't know that you're Paul Slickey?
JACK: You know what her father and the Great Man feel about each other. She'd cut my allowance if it came out.
JO: Your allowance?
JACK: You know me, kid. I have to live big! [13]

The last line tempts one to give Osborne the benefit of the doubt. But the exposition does turn out to have served a purpose on its own account. For after the cinematic send-up, a phone call from Oakham's boss introduces the theme which in the course of the action is to assume centrality—that of Lord Mortlake's dying struggle against the Inland Revenue. The action switches to Mortlake Hall, and the transition is marked by what looks at first like a lead-in to another episode of burlesque:

Hallelujah Productions present in association with Gay
Theatre Limited, Dame Penelope Smart and Sir Wilfred
Childs in "This is our World" by Beaumont Edner. Time:
The Present. An early evening in April. Place: a bedroom
in Mortlake Hall. [19]

There are, sure enough, certain parodistic elements in the
scenes which follow. Lady Mortlake, for example, is a
"magnificently gracious" well-made mummy, who looks like
"one of those incomparable actresses who make incomparable
entrances from the french windows, bring on half a florist's
shop with them and then spend most of the play arranging
them wittily and ignoring the plot." [24]
But this gloss of Deirdre's upon her mother's appearance
also suggests a dramatist uncertain of the force with which he
has made his visual point. Not surprisingly, for Osborne
slips in and out of the burlesque vein at will—as in the
following conversation:

LORD MORTLAKE: Gad, Ethel, you haven't changed much.
MRS GILTEDGE-WHYTE: Haven't I, Freddie?
LORD MORTLAKE: As damned attractive as ever. That girl
who was in here just now—is she—?
MRS GILTEDGE-WHYTE: Yes, Freddie, our daughter. . . .
LORD MORTLAKE: Good heavens, what a careless pleasure-
loving cad I was.
MRS GILTEDGE-WHYTE: Not at all, you were most serious
and after all it was hardly your fault.
LORD MORTLAKE: Of course it was my fault. . . . Whose
fault do you think it was—the Lord Chamberlain's?
MRS GILTEDGE-WHYTE: What I meant was, that the young
people nowadays have access to knowledge which was
denied to us—knowledge which I believe they take advantage of quite freely. [65]

The dialogue here begins as parody, merges into sarcasm, and ends up as a fairly straightforward reflection on changing sexual mores. And then there is the long exercise in cross-purpose between Michael and Deirdre, he talking blandly about the difficulties of the estate, she about the love-affair she supposes him to have rumbled—and here the confusion is stretched to literally farcical lengths. [26–8] As so often in *Slickey*, the characters are remoulded into whatever shape the dramatist's immediate whim dictates.

And Osborne is not even very sure of the object of his contempt, for his attack continues to veer as disconcertingly between the governing classes and the governed as it did in the opening number. Thus, consider the confusion of authorial point-of-view in the following speech of Michael's, in one of his silly-ass moods, about his failure to get into parliament:

> Couldn't understand it. I based almost my entire campaign on giving the H-bomb to the Germans. Half the town was destroyed in air raids during the war, so I thought they would have a particular interest in foreign policy. I'm afraid the electorate can be very irresponsible at times. You know, Lesley, I feel very strongly about all this, I can tell you. [47]

Of course, the heavy-handed juxtaposition of the two opening sentences over-anticipates the sense of the joke. More to the present point, however, is one's feeling that a satirist cannot effectively accuse the electorate of moronic gullibility half the time—and then commend, when it suits his purpose, their sensible opposition to German rearmament, in the face of damn-fool politicians who couldn't, on this evidence, manipulate cheese into a mousetrap.

It is its *double* inconsistency, then—of formal tone, and of satiric standpoint—that flaws *Paul Slickey*, rather than the

minutiae of its discursive social criticism. True, its original
failure was apparently abetted by its audience's inability to
perceive irony in a song with the delicate refrain *We're Going
to Screw, Screw, Screw the Income Tax Man.* [48–9] But that
this lyric mounts an attack upon the materialistic obsessions
of the highly-taxed, rather than constituting the rich
dramatist's slur upon the revenue inspectorate for which
it was mistaken is, in context, evident enough: and the
jazz funeral of Lord Mortlake [71–2] is equally clearly
directed against the debasement of death rather than religion
itself, as some critics suspected. But these misconceptions
were in one sense understandable, for they were symptomatic of a more subtle and pervasive failure of communication. Osborne's medium, in short, simply couldn't contain its
profusion of messages.

A *Tom Thumb* treatment of the modern musical might
well have succeeded. So too might a sourer sort of anti-
musical, or a ballad-play on the lines of *Happy End* or *The
Threepenny Opera.* But a conventionally plotted and irrelevantly choreographed musical-comedy made too many
incidental demands of a formal kind—for romantic mis-
understandings, for choruses, for dancers, for the hasty
last-minute looping of loose-ends—not to have constricted
Osborne's satirical purpose. What remained were some odd
songs, and some occasional bursts of repartee, which were
isolatively effective. A few of the less verbally constipated
lyrics made their points—Mrs Giltedge-Whyte accidentally
monopolising the best songs in the show, *Bring Back the Axe*
[34–5] and *I Want to Hear About Beautiful Things*, [65–6]
which alike flayed the muddled sentiment and sadism
thought to typify the rampant females of the Tory Party's
rank and file.

Of the spoken dialogue, the best is almost invariably the
least heavily pointed:

DEIRDRE: Mummy, I wish you wouldn't encourage Michael with his political career. I'd so much rather he did a job of work.

LADY MORTLAKE: I suppose he could take a few directorships.

DEIRDRE: But darling, that wouldn't keep his *mind* occupied. Antonia's husband has got seventeen directorships and he hangs about the house all day making model boats. She says it's hell! [32]

Those model boats couldn't be bettered in the bathetic wake of the seventeen directorships. But the technique even here is characteristic of a careful *setting-up* of dialogue and situation as stool-pigeons for Osborne's satirical shotgun, which splays out its pellets at journalists and politicians, debs and plebs, exploiters and exploited in a generally wasteful fashion.

That my own criticisms bear little resemblance to those levelled against *The World of Paul Slickey* at the time of its first performance—at the height of the never-had-it-so-good period in British politics—perhaps suggests the essentially occasional nature of the piece. It attacked a kind of "ultimate journalist" even then on the decline—and perhaps it even helped to speed that decline in some complicated and contradictory way. It alluded to a "state of armed conflict" [30]—a phrase which will presumably lose its ironic force as soon as the Suez affair is forgotten. And it forced the most unlikely characters to campaign for stage censorship or to find an outlet in incest. It is, in short, rather a muddle.

Technically, though, it did finally force Osborne out of his naturalistic straitjacket. And perhaps it helped to convince him of his incapacity as a lyric writer—and as a director of his own plays. At least, he has experimented in neither of these latter directions since. Certainly, *Slickey* suggested something about Osborne's artistic makeup that *Plays for*

England was to confirm: that his work does serve a therapeutic purpose, by enabling him to lash his enemies, real or
supposed, at least to his own satisfaction. His capacity for
rhetoric tends to make one forget the ease with which he can
be hurt—as he felt himself hurt at this time by journalistic
distortion. *The World of Paul Slickey* salved a wound which,
imaginary or not, was deeply felt. That accomplished, he
could turn to more serious matters—for Osborne is essentially a "serious" dramatist, as opposed to the funny one he
failed to be in *Paul Slickey*. But in between *Slickey* and the
Plays for England—his next exercises in therapeutic drama—
came *A Subject of Scandal and Concern* and *Luther*. And these
two works looked back not in anger, but in an attempt to
relate the lessons of the past to the needs of the present.

5

A Subject of Scandal and Concern

A SUBJECT OF SCANDAL AND CONCERN was written for television, and the prehistory of its production was not a happy one. Osborne has written nothing further for the medium, and even chose to offer the printed text of his play in a three-act form, though he retained the technical details of its television presentation.[19] On stage, it scarcely occupies more time than a longish one-acter. But Osborne's divisions are logical, for *A Subject of Scandal and Concern* does resemble a truncated full-length piece—at least, more than it does the kind of vignette one would expect to see attempted within such a limited framework. As the text stands, its first act traces the events which culminate in the trial of George Holyoake for blasphemy. The second act concerns the courtroom proceedings, and the third the aftermath of Holyoake's conviction and imprisonment. Osborne's problem was evidently to scale-down the substance of a three-hour action to fit a television drama-slot.

The last person to be imprisoned in this country for taking the name of his god allegedly in vain, George Holyoake,[20] a young and impoverished teacher, actually stood trial early in the reign of Queen Victoria—and the flavour of this period Osborne recaptures as much in his slightly formalised dialogue as in the moral attitudes it embodies. This is a representative snatch of conversation between Holyoake and his wife:

MRS HOLYOAKE: Oh, you are no speaker, and it's idle to

pretend otherwise . . . but you will try your best. I am
sorry.

HOLYOAKE: You are very patient.

MRS HOLYOAKE: You will always recognise your duty and
there it is. We shall all manage. . . . Forgive me, but you
are not an easy man, and I am so anxious for the future.

HOLYOAKE: Please try to be patient. I, too, am anxious. [15]

Only one of nine chances to ellide a collocated pronoun and
verb is taken here, and the stilted explicitness of the closing
exchange heightens one's sense of historical period as well as
characterising Holyoake's personal scrupulousness of expression. But neither Mrs Holyoake nor any character other
than her husband is more than sketched-in, and some—such
as his unsympathetic brother-in-law [18]—appear only in
brief shots of thirty seconds or so.

The purpose of the proliferation of bit-players is apparently
to emphasise Holyoake's personal isolation in a world of
passers-by. Even his wife finally turns against him, and few
of his other antagonists make any attempt at understanding
his position: but he does not react to their failures in the
vituperative manner of a Jimmy Porter. Of all Osborne's
heroes before Luther, he is the most withdrawn, and the one
who finds most difficulty in communicating—at times quite
literally, for he has a nervous impediment in his speech. And,
as if to distance his audience still further from the introverted
Holyoake, Osborne introduces a latter-day narrator who
comments, somewhat condescendingly, on the progress of the
action. This distancing-device was made slightly ambiguous
in the original production by the casting of John Freeman—
then best known as a television interviewer somewhat
astringent in his questioning techniques—as the narrator,
his everyday employment thus posing a Pirandellian
problem as to the nature of his "reality".

There is no such complication in the narrator's verbal manner, however. His attitude to his audience is one of ill-concealed contempt:

> What you are about to see is a straightforward account of an obscure event in the history of your—well my—country. I shall simply fill in with incidental but necessary information, like one of your own television chairmen in fact. You will not really be troubled with anything unfamiliar. I hope you have been reassured. [11]

The narrator's style, as here, combines curtness with a sort of grammatical puritanism: and technically, of course, Osborne's use of this character to provide "incidental but necessary information" solves all his expository troubles. Dramatically, he functions less consistently. How far his ill manners are merely in character, and how far they reflect an author doubtful of his own feelings towards a mass audience, thus remains uncertain.

In spite of its extreme compression, *A Subject of Scandal and Concern* suffers from certain constructional weaknesses. In some ways it reads rather better than it acts: for example, the slight distortions and perversions of Holyoake's crucially "blasphemous" answer to an end-of-lecture question, as reported in an antagonistic newspaper, are probably lost in the immediacy of production—deliberately glossed though they are by the narrator in his concluding comment that the "methods of newspaper morality have changed very little". [17–18] But after accompanying the action to this point— about half-way through the first act—the narrator is reduced to making perfunctory, sound-only appearances until the end of the play. At this stage, he is called upon to point a moral— or rather the absence of a moral. Since his appearances are interruptive at the beginning of the play, the changeover to a consecutively "dramatic" presentation creates a certain dissonance: for the action, having been initiated self-consciously, tends to get caught up in itself as Holyoake's trial progresses. A pseudo-documentary play becomes a courtroom-drama.

Similarly, it is hard to tell whether the climactic loose-ends —such as the well-made dramatist of *George Dillon* and *Look Back in Anger* had been anxious to avoid—are deliberate, or the products of carelessly wielded scissors-and-paste. Why, for example, is the prosecution witness Bertram—alleged by Holyoake to have gained mightily in glibness since his magisterial examination [29]—not actually *seen* during that initial hearing? Why, in so short a play, are a number of procedural quibbles allowed to hold up the courtroom action, when ultimately its theme is not legalistic, but moral? What is the point of opening the third act on a bloody-bells motif [39]—disconcertingly reminiscent of *Look Back in Anger* —which never recurs, and which contributes nothing to the action? And what purpose is served by the altercation in jail between Holyoake and his chaplain, in which the relative acceptability of a prison-issue bible and one bound in calf is the sole point at issue? [41]

The point may, indeed, be that there is no point, for the play is closed by the narrator on a note of careful inconclusiveness:

This is a time when people demand from entertainments what they call a "solution". They expect to have their little solution rattling away down there in the middle of the play like a motto in a Christmas cracker.... For those who seek information, it has been put before you. If it is meaning you are looking for, then you must start collecting for yourself. And what would you say is the moral then...? If you are waiting for the commercial, it is probably this:

you cannot live by bread alone. You must have jam—even if it is mixed with another man's blood. [46]

This slightly macabre image admittedly sets off resonances of its own: but it is not possible to take any of the narrator's assertions at their face value, for *A Subject of Scandal and Concern* is not, in fact, an "entertainment", but one of the most intellectually-oriented of Osborne's plays. It is not, of course, any the worse for that: but the mental challenge involved in co-ordinating the "information"—a challenge which the alienating presence of the narrator at once makes explicit and acceptable—*does* oblige the viewer to consider his own "solution". The problem is not initially one of settling on a convenient answer, however, but of deciding what has to be solved.

What, in short, is the play about? Osborne chooses to present the issue of religious persecution not in terms of inquisitions or of charred stakes, but in terms of judicial proceedings—which are, as Holyoake says,

no more than the poor rags of former persecutions. In this age, as often as men introduce new benefits so do others try to bring back old evils. Gentlemen, what is this p-rosecution? [32]

What is it indeed? A symptom, as Holyoake goes on to suggest, of that "strange infirmity in English minds which makes them accept a bad principle which they, as Englishmen, are no longer bad enough to put into practice"? Perhaps: but Osborne takes care to introduce a priestly zealot into Holyoake's cell who *does* mourn that "the day has gone when we might send you *and* Mr Owen *and* Mr Southwell to the stake". [22] This implies only that Mrs Giltedge-Whyte's axe has been brought back with a vengeance.

Yet Holyoake himself makes clear what has retrospectively proved to be the case—that his was indeed "an antiquated accusation". [33] As antiquated, one might ask as the more frenetic refutations of Osborne's own anti-monarchism? The analogy is tempting, but tangential: for the play itself is less dependent on its central character functioning even partially as an authorial mouthpiece than any of its predecessors. There is only one occasion on which Osborne seems to be putting his own words into the mouth of Holyoake, who in matters of personal morality is as ultra-respectable as his reformist zeal is distinctively Victorian. Yet of Christianity he is made to say:

I do not deny the goodness that is in it but I deny that it is more than a part of goodness. It is passive and obedient. "Thou shalt not" has precedence over "thou shalt". It has always feared the flesh and so it flees from life. It holds out hope of Heaven and the threat of Hell, indulging the fear in individual men, offering an investment instead of a contest. [35]

"It has always feared the flesh and so it flees from life" evokes a startlingly different Holyoake from the paterfamilias lecturing at the mechanics institute. And the wrongness of tone only jars because Holyoake does come consistently alive in his other, less revolutionary moods. He is, indeed, a man who flies "from brawling like a cat from the water", [15] and who struggles only painfully towards the eventual moral —though not legal—triumph of his own defence.

Of all the early Osborne heroes, Holyoake is unique not only in his introversion but, paradoxically, in the public notoriety which forces him to confront his own isola-tion. But he too is "exceptional", knowing that he is "alone in this matter and will remain so." Which is why he is determined, in spite of his impediment, to conduct his own defence:

> It is from no disrespect to the Bar that I did not employ counsel, but because they are unable to enter into my motives. There is a magic circle of orthodoxy they will not step out of. [31]

And this surely comes close to suggesting the reason for Osborne's selection of the *final* prosecution for blasphemy as his subject—his conviction that a "magic circle of orthodoxy" effectively constricts those freedoms which have perhaps been granted theoretically, yet whose exercise still stamps a man "exceptional".

It must, of course, be added that the play does not proceed to hammer home any such "trimmed-off explanation". Its third act is an apparently intentional hotch-potch of un-related events. The prisoner is plagued by bells. He conceals the "itch"—for fear of its cure-by-brimstone. And he learns of the deathbed conversion of his friend Southwell, of the death of his own daughter, and of his wife's increasing conviction of the sinfulness of denying her a Christian burial. Is Holyoake wrong to refuse his wife this small solace? What is the effect of the chaplain's lengthy supplication for his soul, which immediately precedes the play's anti-climax? [45–6] No answer is suggested to either question—a matter of evident relish to the narrator, as his refusal to propose any "little solution rattling away down there in the centre of the play" bears eloquent witness. His imagery is indeed im-pressive—until one realises that it begs not a moral but a *human* question.

A prison sentence presumably does have its effects, for better or worse, upon Holyoake himself: and his immediate confused response to the experience is set down in some detail. But what of its aftermath? Nothing. Holyoake walks through the prison gates "into the cold December early morning", and the governor's laughter follows him. [46] It is a pity that the play has nothing better to offer than a cine-matic cliché in climactic proof of its complexity: for *A Subject of Scandal and Concern* is full of material of genuine dramatic potential. Holyoake himself is powerfully yet economically sketched in, and the impression of his increasing isolation is conveyed with dramatic dignity and technical assurance. And then, like a reactionary magistrate pontificating on the self-sufficiency of punishment, Osborne seems to lose interest in his prisoner as soon as he has done his time.

Perhaps the trouble is that—in spite and because of the conventions shaping it—*A Subject of Scandal and Concern* is simply not long enough. It has been whittled down to a size acceptable to a television schedule—yet it contains the kernel of a full-length play, struggling for room to grow and develop. Neither its setting nor its formal construction would have been difficult to adapt to the stage, and one rather wishes that Osborne—assuming his disillusionment with television—had undertaken such an adaptation, and the expansion it would have made possible. As it is, this remains an intriguing but flawed attempt at character-drawing—one which is flawed by a choice of canvas better suited to caricature than to the detailed portrait it just begins to suggest.

6

Luther

LUTHER is a play about physical and spiritual purgatory on earth. The evacuation of the bowels and the purification of the church are thus conceived as parallel processes in the life of the eponymous hero. But historical-cum-psychological enquiries into the actual nature of Martin Luther's obsession with his chronic constipation are of no more than marginal relevance to the play, for Osborne's interpretation of history is of the whig variety—an approach to the past which is modified by the attitudes it has subsequently helped to shape. *Luther* is thus intended to throw as much light on the problems of the present as on the historical conflict it chronicles: and the tradition of whig history plays, stretching from the works of the Wakefield Master to *Henry V*, and from *Saint Joan* to *Left-Handed Liberty*, suggests forcefully enough that the distinction is not one of form but of emphasis. For in style *Luther*, which reached the Royal Court in July 1961, and enjoyed a lengthy transfer to the Phoenix Theatre, is idio-syncratically the work of John Osborne. It is *not* an epic—in spite of those critics who persist in regarding a common-man who "briefly barks the time and place" of the action as an infallible sign of Brechtian heresy, rather than as a time-saving device. This, anyway, is all that justifies—but for one exceptional scene—the knight's narrative function.

Luther is of all Osborne's plays the one which states its subject least equivocally in its title[21]. And this subject—the isolation of a single man—is, of course, common to almost all the dramatist's work. It is also self-evidently unsuited to the wider-ranging purposes of epic—except in its strictest Aristotelian sense as a narrative that happens to be wide-ranging in *time*. But I don't want to expend too much space on the purely corrective business of asserting that *Luther* is not (as in praise or blame it has usually been dubbed) a Brechtian play. So a brief note by Brecht himself on the qualities which distinguish the epic from the conventionally "dramatic" form must suffice:

> This is no place to explain how the opposition of epic and dramatic lost its rigidity after having long been held to be irreconcilable. Let us just point out that the technical advances alone were enough to permit the stage to incorporate an element of narrative in its dramatic productions. . . . The most important transactions between people could no longer be shown simply by personifying the motive forces or subjecting the characters to invisible metaphysical powers.
>
> To make these transactions intelligible the environment in which the people lived had to be brought to bear in a big and "significant" way.
>
> This environment had of course been shown in the existing drama, but only as seen from the central figure's point of view, and not as an independent element. It was defined by the hero's reactions to it. It was seen as a storm can be seen when one sees the ships on a sheet of water unfolding their sails, and the sails filling out. In the epic theatre it was to appear standing on its own.[22]

Earlier Brecht had described the epic theatre as appealing "less to the feelings than to the spectator's reason".[23] According to such criteria, *Luther* is indisputably "dramatic" rather than epic. In particular, the hero's environment is indeed defined by his reactions to it, and the play's primary appeal is indeed emotional rather than rational. Like all Osborne's work, *Luther* is *intended* to be a lesson in feeling. It is not primarily a history play—and least of all is it an exercise in the dialectics of reformation theology.

The distinction between "epic" and "dramatic" is not, of course, an evaluative one. It does have to be determined, all the same, whether those very elements which have confused critics into describing the play's dramaturgy as Brechtian do not in themselves detract from its actual "dramatic" qualities. Certainly, the two or three episodes which are characterised by epic self-containment serve paradoxically to underline the interdependence of the remaining scenes in the play—because it is precisely those few scenes which do *not* depend upon Luther's centrifugal force which also begin to assume an epic quality. First of all, there is Tetzel's indulgence-touting. This is an isolated exercise in travesty which—though it serves its immediate purpose of impressing upon an audience one of Martin's main doctrinal differences with his church—jars oddly with the marginally heightened but historically right-sounding prose of the surrounding scenes:

Take a good look. There isn't one sin so big that one of these letters can't remit it. I challenge any one here, any member of this audience, to present me with a sin, anything, any kind of sin, I don't care what it is, that I can't settle for him with one of these precious little envelopes. Why, if any one had ever offered violence to the Blessed Virgin Mary, Mother of God, if he'd only pay up—as long as he paid up all he could—he'd find himself forgiven. You think I'm exaggerating? You do, do you? Well, I'm authorised to go even further than that. Not only am I empowered to give you these letters of pardon for the sins you've already committed, I can give you pardon for those

D

sins you haven't even committed (*pause . . . then slowly*) but, which, however you *intend* to commit! [49–50]

This comes close stylistically to the later scene in the hunting lodge, during which the pope fiddles while Martin's letter of appeal burns. [75–8] And this, in turn, is related to the knight's solo-spot, which, though idiomatically consistent and controlled, scarcely suffices even as a discursive statement of Luther's role in fomenting and subsequently helping to crush the Peasant's Revot—although the time-lag preceding it would make such a statement both permissible and purposeful. [86–8]

The knight's scene has the quality described by Tim in *Under Plain Cover* as "elliptical elastical"—and its evasiveness about examining the practical, human consequences of Martin's heresy is typical. The *theoretical* dangers of his reformist aims have been thrashed out, in general terms, in the dispute between a still-just-faithful Martin and the papal legate Cajetan—and the latter's warning of the disintegration which a successful challenge to the church's authority will bring in its wake is given this climactic emphasis:

You know, a time will come when a man will no longer be able to say, "I speak Latin and am a Christian" and go his way in peace. There will come frontiers, frontiers of all kinds—between men—and there'll be no end to them. [74]

But the point made here is never explored or exemplified. A four-year gap follows Martin's refusal to retract at the Diet of Worms—the gap that creates the narrative necessity for the knight's retrospection. Here, as throughout the play, the substance of the episode is thus a statement of a fully-developed situation. Luther is never seen to *change*—least of all from the sweating revolutionary of the penultimate scene to the domesticated cleric entertaining an old friend, on whom the final curtain rather cursorily falls. Neither—and perhaps this is why the knight's scene fails to convince—is he seen to have the quality of changing *other* men. Luther is not so much a character, in short, as a collection of introverted characteristics, physical and mental, which demand realisation psychologically as well as severally.

Constipation, epilepsy and sweat distinguish Luther bodily, and determine also his mental condition—for he is conceived much more fully as a private man hemmed-in by his own physicality than as a politico-religious animal. The assurance of the portraiture at this level is consistent, albeit segmented in its chronological development. Certainly, Osborne notes an *intended* change in stylistic emphasis between the first and second of his three acts:

> After the intense private interior of Act One, with its outer darkness and rich, personal objects, the physical effect from now on should be more intricate, general, less personal; sweeping, concerned with men in time rather than particular man in the unconscious; caricature not portraiture, like the popular woodcuts of the period. . . . [46]

But things don't work out quite like this. The elements of caricature are there, sure enough—and as if to assert Osborne's point, the very next scene after his authorial note is Tetzel's *tour de force* of spiritual salesmanship. But the transition which follows is to the Eremite cloister, which provides a setting for the lengthy dialogue between Martin and Staupitz, Vicar General of the Augustinian Order.

[52–60] A certain difference in tenor between this scene and the first act is admittedly achieved, but this is a matter of changed environment—from monastery to monastery-garden, as it were—and not of any differences in rendering the characters.

A fundamental change does derive from the rounding-out and softening of Martin's own character, but this is not a *stylistic* modification. It is, however, only the first of several occasions on which such a change—marking here no less than a decade in time—is taken for granted. Thus, the *effects* on Martin's character of the forces which have been influencing him during the blank years are made clear enough. But the existence and gradual working of these forces is merely assumed—as also is the slow recognition of Martin's intellectual abilities, and the shaking-off of that obsession with the outward forms of religion which was so marked at the beginning of the play.

The first act is also the most impressive in performance, thanks to the sure-fire effect of its monastic trimmings. The vignette on which the curtain rises is of a monk, watched by his uncomprehending father, caught up in the ritual of his final vows. [13–4] The visual statement is self-explanatory, saving Osborne his old expository troubles: the play begins, as it were, at Martin's commitment to a new beginning. Even so, Osborne can't resist an ostensibly casual explanation of the presence of Lucas, an old friend of Martin's father, Hans. Lucas is functionally quite acceptable as a foil to his more outspoken comrade: but Osborne goes out of his way to reveal that he is also the father of a girl Martin might have married. [15] The clumsiness is slight, but characteristic: for no more is heard of Martin's lost love.

Neither, come to that, is much more heard or anything seen of Hans and Lucas after the first act. And this is strange, for Hans's colloquial confrontations, of which the last and longest is with his son, serve a distinct dramatic purpose, besides leavening the ritualistic tone—that of clarifying the nature of the relationship between father and son, and of stressing its importance in Martin's development:

HANS: What do you think it is makes you different? Other men are all right, aren't they? You were stubborn, you were always stubborn, you've always had to resist, haven't you?

MARTIN: You disappointed me too, and not just a few times, but at some time of every day I ever remember hearing or seeing you, but, as you say, maybe that was also no different from any other boy. But I loved you the best. It was always *you* I wanted. I wanted your love more than anyone's, and if anyone was to hold me, I wanted it to be you. Funnily enough, my mother disappointed me the most, and I loved her less, much less. She made a gap which no one else could have filled, but all she could do was make it bigger, bigger and more unbearable. [43]

The point here hinted at is explicated almost too clearly a few exchanges later:

HANS: I thought you were blaming your mother and me for your damned monkery!

MARTIN: Perhaps I should. [44]

"What do you think it is makes you different?" Hans has asked: and the play at this point seems all set to explore some tentative answers to his bewildered question, and to its corollary: "Do you know why? Lucas: Why? What made him do it?" [16–17]

The first act, sure enough, traces back some of the

symptoms of Martin's self-doubt to the deficiencies of his own childhood:

> Somewhere, in the body of a child, Satan foresaw in me what I'm suffering now. That's why he prepares open pits for me, and all kinds of tricks to bring me down, so that I keep wondering if I'm the only man living who's baited, and surrounded by dreams, and afraid to move. [30]

Now this is to become a recurrent theme, which is first reiterated at the end of the scene in which the foregoing lines occur—when, its visual symbolism clarifying the significance of the motif, Martin "advances towards the audience . . . carrying a naked child". [30] So if the responsibility of Hans for Martin's childhood-orientation is really as crucial as his presence and function in the first act seem to suggest, it's only appropriate that he should begin to seem, after Luther himself, the most fully-developed person in the play—and this, it's worth noting, in an act allegedly of "outer darkness". Osborne even indulges his penchant for pen-portraiture in introducing him into the script:

> It is Martin's father, a stocky man wired throughout with a miner's muscle, lower-middle class, on his way to become a small, primitive capitalist; bewildered, full of pride and resentment. [14]

Hans, then, like so many of Osborne's more interesting characters, hides his feelings behind a persona, just occasionally ceasing, in those rare moments of self-doubt, to play the adopted, aggressive role he has chosen.

That this role has, however, been as important as the

reality in the relationship between Hans and his son is
confirmed in their conversation together—and even reflected
in the terms Osborne uses to describe this conversation, Hans
variously "manoeuvring for position" [34] or "determined
not to lose the initiative". [35] And that the father has a fair
idea of his son's capacity for causing disruption is indicated
by his remarks to Martin's brother monks:

> Wouldn't you say then—I'm not saying this in any crit-
> icism, mind, but because I'm just interested, naturally, in
> the circumstances—but wouldn't you say that one bad
> monk, say for instance, one really monster sized, roaring
> great bitch of a monk, if he really got going, couldn't he
> get his order such a reputation that eventually, it might
> even have to go into—what do they call it now—liquida-
> tion. That's it. Liquidation. [31–2]

If the dramatic irony here is Osborne's, it is simply unsubtle.
But if it is Hans's—as by the elliptical, cautious manner of its
phrasing it would appear to be—then the acuteness of his
understanding of his son is further substantiated. And so,
incidentally, is Osborne's sympathetic interest in this latest
representative of an older, disoriented generation. But the
father-son relationship ends abruptly at the close of the first
act, not only in terms of physical contact—which the ensuing gap of a decade dictates—but even in terms of assimilated influence.

And it is only at this later stage—in contradiction of
Osborne's intended change of emphasis, but in consequence
of the focus-concentrating effects of the transition from
portraiture to caricature in the realisation of environment—
that Martin emerges as the central figure of the play. But the
dialectics in which he now engages for scene after scene—
various shifting figures on the outskirts of the action serving

successively as antagonists—seem to be dissociated from his search for personal salvation, whereas his verbal skirmishing with Hans was as inextricably bound up with his religion as with his relation. The theological and the personal themes begin to diverge. We witness little after the first act of the inner evolution of Martin's spiritual struggle: for in his outward conflicts with others he is arguing from a basis of fully formed beliefs.

In the first act, then, Martin's personal and religious struggles were interdependent—marked by the opening stress laid upon his freedom of choice, [13] and later by the continuous conflict between his desire to humiliate his own pride and his troubled sense of the validity of his hubristically independent thinking. Thus:

BROTHER WEINAND: Father Nathin told me he had to punish you only the day before yesterday because you were in some ridiculous state of hysteria, all over some verse in Proverbs or something.
MARTIN: "Know thou the state of thy flocks."
BROTHER WEINAND: And all over the interpretation of one word apparently. When will you ever learn? You must know what you're doing. Some of the brothers laugh quite openly at you, you and your over-stimulated conscience. Which is wrong of them, I know, but you must be able to see why.
MARTIN: It's the single words that trouble me. [26–7]

In this next passage, Martin is feeling towards the protestant concern for an unmediated contact with God, just as the earlier exchanges suggested the new clarity with which he needed to analyse the scriptures:

When I entered the monastery, I wanted to speak to God

directly, you see. Without any embarrassment, I wanted
to speak to him myself, but when it came to it, I dried up—
as I always have. [38]

A few moments later Martin is "directly" asking his father
why he hates him leading a monastic life: religious and
personal doubts are inseparable. But they *are* thereafter
separated out: the element of monastic ritual, for example,
is necessarily abandoned, but it is not succeeded by any
interest in the development of reformed modes of worship.
And this marks Osborne's apparent loss of interest in the
progress of Martin as a protestant, which in consequence
becomes incidental and almost irrelevant to the growth of
Martin as a man.

This is possibly indicative of a failure on Osborne's part to
assimilate all his available source material—mainly garnered
from the psycho-analytical study *Young Man Luther*, by Erik
H. Erikson, which was published two years before *Luther* was
first staged.[24] In the attempt to realise Luther's human
complexity within three hours of stage-time, loose ends have
been left, and themes no sooner suggested than arbitrarily
abandoned—as are the successive issues of theological debate,
and the political impact of Luther's teaching, besides the
father-son relationship. Just one theme makes the play and
the person whole. That is the theme of physicality—which is
relentlessly pursued in the mental processes of an anally-
obsessed neurotic, who is subject to profuse sweating, chronic
constipation, and epileptic fits. And who also just happened
to be a religious reformer.

If only Osborne had matched his style to his dominant
subject matter, all might have been well. As it is, *Luther* is
neither epic nor psychological drama, though it is certainly
more nearly and more consistently the latter. What remains
is an exercise in scatology. Religion becomes a direct

manifestation of Luther's physical condition, both in his own estimation:

> I'm like a ripe stool in the world's straining anus, and at any moment we're about to let each other go. [55]

And in the estimation of his friends:

> Constipated? There's always something the matter with you, Brother Martin. If it's not the gripes, insomnia, or faith and works, it's boils or indigestion or some kind of belly-ache you've got. [55]

Constipation—and faith-and-works. Divine revelation has a direct relationship with physical purgation:

> I thought of the righteousness of God, and wished his gospel had never been put to paper for men to read; who demanded my love and made it impossible to return it. And I sat in my heap of pain until the words emerged and opened out. "The just shall live by faith." My pain vanished, my bowels flushed and I could get up. I could see the life I'd lost. No man is just because he does just works. The works are just if the man is just. [63]

And so on. It is at such moments as these—when the metaphors merge with the mentality of the man—that Osborne's customary control over language asserts itself, and Luther's private pain pours out in anally-obsessed verbiage. His *public* utterances, similarly expressed, exert comparable theatrical power: but they contain no clue to Martin's power of *political* compulsion. Far from being concerned with "men in time", the final acts thus continue to explore an "intense private interior"—in an all too apt freudian sense!

To pursue an excremental image-hunt would be simple but tedious. Martin is not the only one who has "allegorised going to the lavatory", and his own comment on the deficiency of the exercise is equally pertinent as a criticism of Osborne's "public" play. For

> allegories aren't much help in theology—except to decorate a house that's been already built by argument. [52-3]

Osborne has allegorised convincingly, but argued cursorily. His failure to *apply* his anal imagery—to sustain the connection between constipation and nonconformity at a cerebral level—is thus his own as well as Luther's. His "virgin heretic" lives in his sweat-soaked virginity, but not in his heresy. And as a consequence *Luther* is just half the play it might have been.

7

Plays for England

THESE TWO playlets were probably as necessary, in their
ways, as palliatives to Osborne's self-esteem as *The World of
Paul Slickey*: and they were not much better received.
Flawed exercises in exaggeration, both belong to that dusty
top-shelf of an author's writings which Shaw once labelled
his *Trifles and Tomfooleries*—forgiven and perhaps best
forgotten plays on themes which seemed important or
promising at the time, yet which somehow turned out
trivial.

Osborne not only chose ill-considered subjects, but treated
them with an unwise and forced flippancy. For he has never
been a subtle humourist. His laughter, like his despair, tends
to be overweening—as intentionally brash as Archie's
music-hall turns in *The Entertainer*, or as accidentally so as
Luther's "attempts at lightness". Osborne's fondness for the
comic style of Ken Dodd suggests well enough his own
approach to the business of being funny. In *Plays for England*,
however, he at least concentrates his comedy on particular
dramatic targets—whereas in *Slickey* he had let fly indis-
criminately in all directions. The faults of these playlets are
rather different: in their case, it is more as if Osborne had
taken a brace of blunderbusses to lay siege to a semi-
detached doll's house. His new targets—royalty-worship in
The Blood of the Bambergs, and press interference in *Under
Plain Cover*—were too puny for his big batteries to take proper
aim. Perhaps pop-guns, in the form of revue-sketches, would
have served his purpose better.

One or two of Osborne's references in *The Blood of the Bambergs* to the economics of the monarchical system may illustrate my point. The foreman of a firm of royal-route constructors, interviewed on the eve of that "most solemn occasion in our national life", [14] Princesss Melanie's marriage to Prince Wilhelm of the House of Bamberg,[25] replies to one question as follows:

> I myself, just in my section mind you, I have calculated that during the past seventeen years in which I have had the honour to do this job, I could have built, using the same materials and labour, you understand, twenty-seven secondary modern schools and one million two hundred thousand houses. [20]

The idiom of the interviewee—caught up in his own adverbial clauses—is nicely echoed: but the final equation is simply too absurd to work as satire.

Later it emerges that Prince Wilhelm has been killed in a motoring accident on his way to the wedding—on a highway cleared from one end to the other for his better safety. But the royal show must go on: so a bastard Bamberg, discovered to his own surprise in the person of an Australian press photographer, is chosen for a crash course in consortship. He is bribed into acquiescence:

> After an event such as your wedding, they will almost certainly do something ordinarily unpopular, like cutting the schools programme and *increase* your allowance. . . . And at such time as the Princess should produce an heir, there would be similar arrangements. [48]

This is neither satire nor a single distortion which fits into a consistently gross caricature: it is simply exaggeration to serve an immediate, incidental purpose. So, too, is this ministerial apologia:

> It is, as we all know, a sad fact that these joyous occasions are always and inevitably accompanied by a considerable number of deaths. And I regret to say that these figures have been steadily rising. They even exceed the figure for deaths on the road—and you know how concerned we were about them. We thought *that* was a problem. However, this is the market price of progress and of civilisation. [26]

What one objects to is not the airing of such inflated imaginings, but their sheer arbitrariness. There is an acceptable point in attacking pettily-preoccupied politicians, by making one agree with his interrogator that "the United Socialist Party more or less fought the Election" on the issue of the creation of his Ministry—a Ministry of Royal Occasions. [22] But it is surely no less culpable to be preoccupied purely with the repudiation of such marginal symptoms of social malaise. No dramatist is obliged to write a play on the theme of defence estimates, or to commit himself on the pros and cons of breathalysers. But having *chosen* to take the economic and the supposed human costs of the monarchy as his theme, it should surely have been possible for Osborne to set these in a less distorted perspective. True, it is possible to regard the piece as purely propagandist in intention, and therefore beyond the bounds of such criticism: but even propaganda is at its most effective when it comes uncomfortably closest to the truth. Osborne's distortion, however, is at times so violent as to resemble a pro-monarchist parodying his enemy's arguments—and it takes a writer as subtle as Swift to attempt such twice-removed satire successfully.

The Blood of the Bambergs begins as a television interview, and thus combines its exposition with a well-observed caricature of one of the more parenthetical practitioners in the medium. Consider Osborne's simple but effective technique, in this brief extract from the commentator's preamble. Functionally, it foreshadows the royal fatality:

> It is now, er, by my watch, eight minutes past twelve and according to our report here, the Prince is at this moment speeding along in his car to be in good time at his appointed place tomorrow. As he drives along in his powerful sports car—and the Prince is a very fine, skilful and fast driver, as I have reason to know, I have watched him on several occasions—as he drives along, I wonder what his thoughts are. Well, that we shall never know of course. . . . [21]

And so on. The combination of tortuous yet absent-minded prose which distinguishes the television journalist forced into a fillibuster is exactly caught.

Much of the play might, ironically enough, be better suited to the intimacy of the television screen than to the stage. For if it is to succeed at all, it must do so by the confrontation in close-up of its gallery of modern grotesques—a proximity impossible on stage, in the acreage of the mock-cathedral interior. In fact, John Dexter's original production, staged at the Royal Court in July 1962, did make use of a cinematic insert—and quick cross-cutting by a film camera might better bring out the point of the following kind of exchange:

> WIMPLE: And how many men are involved in this work?
> LEMON: I have under me at the present time nine hundred and forty-seven, that's if my memory serves me right.
> WIMPLE: Nearly a thousand men and what are they?
> LEMON: What do you mean, what are they?
> WIMPLE: I mean what do they do? [17]

This slight crossing of purposes, unobtrusively characterising both the commentator's self-reliant jargon and the builder's mild obtuseness, is a redeeming example of humour whose tartness is exact rather than irrelevantly sour. But Osborne can seldom resist a chance to change hobby-horses in midstream.

> BROWN: Taft, I don't know who you talk to in your job, but has it never struck you as slightly odd, even for a young Prince, that he should divide his time almost exclusively between the barracks and visiting the ballet.
> TAFT: Well, naturally I thought that going to the theatre was a bit eccentric. [33]

Pause for enlightened laughter.

The play's second short act takes place mainly in a private room at the palace, where the newly-blooded Bamberg takes breakfast, and encounters one of his more excessively loyal subjects, who has been secreting herself in the royal laundry chute. She ends up committing suicide when her amorous advances are spurned: and a journalistic acquaintance of the photographer contributes a second corpse to the proceedings, having stumbled on the truth—for which he must naturally be liquidated. Into this mounting atmosphere of extravaganza Osborne propels Princess Melanie, resigned to her fate, and full of wise saws about the functions and the frustrations of the monarchy. The photographer is captivated:

> Being alone with you in this soft, grey light, being so close to you, I suddenly understand the meaning of royalty. I feel the long, thrusting, sexual stimulus of the crown. [68]

But the banal edge is taken off this delicious remark by the genuine dignity with which Osborne unexpectedly endows his princess. As in the case of Paul Slickey—and, indeed, of the anti-heroic newspaperman in *Under Plain Cover*—viciousness personified makes for viciousness modified.

In a brief concluding scene the action reverts to the cathedral, and to a mock television-commentary. Stylistic gear is changed again. The play has thus meandered between the revue-sketch world of its opening and closing scenes into the black comedy of its corpse-strewn wedding, having paused briefly in that other world where Melanie and her instant bridegroom meet—and where something approaching a "real" relationship is struck up between them. Each stylistic expectation is aroused only to be confounded, and the resultant ambiguity dulls the edge of Osborne's ridicule.

The Blood of the Bambergs is the only one of Osborne's plays which lacks an "exceptional" character or characters at its core—for even Jack Oakham in *Slickey* has his alternative role as an upper-class George Dillon, diverted into Fleet Street instead of Tooting Bec. And it is perhaps in this lack, rather than in its ragbag of styles, that its fundamental weakness lies. Osborne seems to need the strong central focus that a hero or anti-hero provides. At least, it is notable that his experiments in style, whether they have been attempts to narrow down his focus (as he was to do most successfully in *Inadmissible Evidence*) or to extend it (as in *A Patriot for Me*), have nevertheless needed the presence of such a strong central character as a precondition of the experiment. *The Blood of the Bambergs*, in default of a hero to hold it together, thus amounts to little more than a sequence of sketches in dissonant styles. And their common theme of royalty-worship instead of serving as a linking-motif actually contributes to the disruption: for the hobby-horse is ridden not by an acceptably eccentric hero, but by a quixotic author tilting at windmills of his own construction.

"And then, of course, there's the obvious influence of Genet," comments Tim, co-hero of *Under Plain Cover*, in the course of a parodied "Critics" discussion on the subject of knickers. [118] Tim's other and better half is Jenny, and this couple are exceptional in the sexual sense—not for the first nor the last time in an Osborne play. They are clothes fantasists—a term which suggests better than clothes *fetishists* the nature of the couple's dependence on a variety of outer and under-garments. For these do not, it appears, serve in themselves as objects of sexual pleasure, but as enhancements of it—as means by which the pair act out fantasy-relationships of unspecified termination. The ambiguity lies in the hints of a sado-masochistic element: but whether this is merely an occasional wayside-halt on the road to orgasm or its invariable turning-point is not made very clear, perhaps deliberately.

The play's opening scenes have an unexpected but entirely appropriate charm. There is tact and lightness of touch in Osborne's exploration of the couple's relationship—and also a recognition of the tenderness that is generated by their fantasies, as it was by Alison and Jimmy Porter's games of bears-and-squirrels. Osborne is at pains, too, to illustrate the way in which reality has to be accommodated by the pair: it is a visit from the postman, and the consequent argument over which of the current repertoire of disguises is least likely to arouse his curiosity, which opens the play. It also, incidentally, makes clear a point that might otherwise have remained too long in doubt—that Tim is not really the doctor he seems, nor Jenny a housemaid. [83–4] The fantasy-world, in short, never *becomes* the real world: so the influence of Genet is not so very obvious after all.

For about two-thirds of its length, *Under Plain Cover* is a duologue, confined within the walls and the world in which Jenny and Tim have chosen to live. Particularly well-conceived is the child-like manner in which they are shown skipping from dream to discussion and back again—a dual-consciousness, as it were, of game-as-game and game-as-reality. These exchanges—in which Jenny is acting as complaisant maidservant to a masterful Tim—are representative:

> TIM: There are plenty of girls just waiting, longing to step into your shoes.
> JENNY: Yes, sir. Oh—is this the nineteen thirties?
> TIM: Yes.
> JENNY: When did you think of that?
> TIM: When do you think? Just now.
> JENNY: Oh, what a good idea! Oh, please, sir. I need the job badly. Dad's still on the dole, and both me brothers are down bad. [90]

And there are, too, intriguing moments when an identity is poised—as a stage-direction puts it [93]—half-way between the reality and the pretence.

The early, "private" part of the play pauses only once in time, to permit some kind of off-stage consummation—and simultaneously to effect a doorstep introduction to a newspaper reporter named Stanley. [98] He is, naturally, of the seediest variety. Even in *The Blood of the Bambergs* Osborne had seized every opportunity for damning the press along with the monarchy—such as the murder of the pseudo-footman presented:

> RUSSELL: He was a journalist.
> WITHERS: Journalist! Good lord!
> TAFT: Well, that's not so bad then, after all. [64]

And now Osborne gets Stanley into conversation with the postman:

POSTMAN: Here, you're Press, aren't you?

REPORTER: Don't tell me *you've* got a grudge. We did you boys rather well over your wage demand, didn't we?

POSTMAN: (*drily*) Thanks, mate. You can carry me sack for me, too, if you like. [99]

Note the assumption—or perhaps the wish fathering the thought—that *everybody* has a grudge against the press. And for the rest of the play it is this grudge which takes control. Tim and Jenny are allowed one more fantasy-scene—culminating in their extended eulogy of knickers of all kinds. And then comes the complicating crunch. The couple are, or so Stanley has been tipped off, really brother and sister as well as husband and wife. [123]

Now had the play proceeded to justify incest as well as sartorial sexuality it could have been judged on terms which —whatever medical or moral questions might have been begged—would have at least seemed self-consistent. Instead the accidental incest is merely a means of displaying the machinations of the gutter press at its worst—its revelation of the relationship "in the public interest", its auction for Jenny's exclusive confessions, even its manipulation of her muddled emotions into an agreement to take a second husband. [125–9] With disconcerting abruptness, the play ceases to bother about its two exceptional human beings. It effectively displaces Tim and Jenny—who are only allocated two further lines apiece, apart from an extract read by Jenny from her ghosted memoirs—in favour of a motley assortment of journalists and wedding-guests, whose activities are linked by the increasingly complex figure of Stanley.

If anything, it is Stanley who takes over the play—and who gets, like Jack Oakham in *Slickey*, an unexpected share of the sympathy. He tries, unavailingly, to prevent a colleague from introducing Tim among the wedding-guests:

STANLEY: Listen, I don't know what you're up to, but I've promised these people a serious nice wedding—not a peep show. And I'm keeping to that.
REPORTER: Well, it's a good twist.
STANLEY: Damn your twist!
REPORTER: Relax, Stanley. You're drunk. You only try to be moral when you're drunk. [131]

This is Osborne getting it both ways with a vengeance. But in consequence of the reunion thus engineered, Jenny returns to Tim—and Stanley, nine years later, discovers them living "in dark seclusion" in their old home. He calls to them through the letter box without evoking any response, and as the curtain falls he "collapses, drunk and miserable. Dead possibly." [134–6] And that's it: a play which begins as a light-textured plea for sexual tolerance ends as a melo-dramatic cautionary-tale about the dangers of journalistic corruption.

The effect of this is not only to split the play in two: its concluding scenes also raise all sorts of unnecessary doubts about its opening. That Tim and Jenny are said to have lived in total privacy for seven years reminds us far too forcibly that their sex-play is *all* we know of their lives. Jenny, who seems not to be fantasising at the time, has mentioned earlier that she works in an office. [105] There are several references to not being able to afford things, and the couple have two babies. And at the time, these naturalistic details give context to occasional, albeit ironic doubts about their mutual-immersion:

TIM: Hey—do you think we're living on relics?
JENNY: Who?
TIM: You and me.
JENNY: Probably.

TIM: So do I. Do you think they're diminishing in some way?

JENNY: What?

TIM: Well, knickers, for instance.

JENNY: No, why should they be?

TIM: You're sure?

JENNY: Quite. Why, aren't you?

TIM: I think so. I ask myself: *am* I diminished? But I can't always be sure. [108]

The quick flow of the dialogue here lends verbal force to the couple's interdependence, and is well integrated into the early mood of the play. The question posed in Tim's last line is, indeed, what the action at this stage seems to be about. And it is attempting nothing so pretentious as an *answer* to that question—merely to probe it with delicacy and compassion.

What is *not* attempted, until the incest-theme is introduced, is any Pirandellian interweaving of the levels of fantasy and reality. Tim and Jenny recognise the boundaries along which they tread, and, indeed, are fully aware of their own isolation:

JENNY: Do you think there are many people like us?

TIM: No. Probably none at all, I expect.

JENNY: Oh, there must be some.

TIM: Well, yes, but probably not two together.

JENNY: You mean just one on their own?

TIM: Yes.

JENNY: How awful. We are lucky.

TIM: I know. [112]

In so far as there can be a final answer to Tim's earlier doubts, it is probably here: and its conviction is reinforced by the mutually-responsive togetherness of the repartee.

So why did Osborne complicate the issue with incest? Such a secondary level of sexual abnormality might be acceptable in farce, or even in high tragedy, in both of which genres excessive turns of the screw are conventional—and acceptable. But here the complication oversteps the formal boundaries which Osborne was at such pains to define in the first part of his play. And, in consequence, its concluding charade acts as a *reductio ad absurdum* of Osborne's argument for tolerance. The incest-theme functions more as an excuse for introducing press-baiting than as an elucidation of Tim and Jenny's personal predicament. A strange play, then, and one which is much more viable than its companion piece: but it has a dying fall.

8

Inadmissible Evidence

OF ALL Osborne's lessons in feeling, *Inadmissible Evidence* has so far been the most impressive. I think it is also the likeliest of his plays to retain an audience in the living theatre—not as folklore, like *Look Back in Anger*, and still less as an advanced-level set-text, like *Luther*, but as a distinctively dramatic experience affording an unusual kind of emotional insight. The mind and the feelings of Osborne's central character—and here the centrality has a particularly precise sense—are probed with an insight that is compassionate yet unyielding. And that character, Bill Maitland, is probably more representative a product of the sixties than Jimmy Porter ever was of the fifties: but his malaise is also more akin to Hamlet's, at once of his own and of all times. For Bill Maitlands go to spiritual seed in every period, drifting into dissociation with their age, and, ultimately, with reality itself.

Inadmissible Evidence, said Bernard Levin, in his review of the original production at the Royal Court in September 1964, was an "attempt to get behind the fashionable theatrical obsession with identity, and grapple with the much more important problems of existence itself". The distinction suggested here is pertinent. Osborne's play poses no metaphysical problems, attempts to construct no absurdist microcosm: rather, it assumes the existence of a recognisable "reality", and sets one man at odds with it. And within two days of time, and the two acts they fill out, it portrays the final stages of his struggle, the acceptance of total isolation.

This is *Waiting for Godot* just before the waiting begins: or, more exactly, the beginning of the waiting coincides with the final curtain of *Inadmissible Evidence*. [115]

The hero of *Inadmissible Evidence*, Bill Maitland, is a solicitor, and the legalistic significance of the play's title is more or less self-explanatory. Its substance is, indeed, the evidence that never reaches court—the body of experience and the accumulation of disappointment which shapes but does not justify one man's motives and actions. *Inadmissible Evidence* is *all* special pleading. Maitland is immersed in self-pity: but the empathetic totality with which an audience comes to comprehend him makes him a worthy subject for their own pity. And the play is structurally as well as sympathetically the best Osborne has written: its stylistic transitions closely shadow changes in the state of Maitland's consciousness, and the solipsistic centrality of the solicitor makes for a functioning of the minor characters which was to remain uniquely successful in Osborne's work—at least until *Hotel in Amsterdam* fitted half a dozen people into its single, unifying but naturalistic friendship.

In one of his stage-directions, Osborne calls for a realisation of the "ambiguity of reality" [63]—a phrase which makes up in exactness what it lacks in euphony. For it is Maitland's increasing sense and eventual acceptance of this ambiguity which gives the play its shape. Archie Rice had been waiting twenty years for the income-tax man. Bill Maitland has spent just about as long wondering when the Law Society is going to catch up with him—not only to avenge a certain lack of scrupulousness about rigging evidence in deserving causes, but also to confront him with his personal failures of conduct and perception.

The play therefore opens during one of Bill's recurrent nightmares—a dream-courtroom, in which he himself is the prisoner in the dock. The surrealist trial is akin to several others in recent dramatic literature—in Irving's *Bells*, in Jan Grossman's version of Kafka's *Trial*, in Jonathan Miller's television *Alice*. That the setting in this case combines the qualities of a courtroom with those of a solicitor's office reflects, psychologically, Maitland's own preconceptions about his guilt. But it also ensures a smooth transition to the reality of that office in the clearer light of day: and this is typical of Osborne's success in adapting his play's formal conditions to its dramatic requirements. The courtroom-scene meets his minimal expository needs, juxtaposing Bill's profession and his precarious mental state. It also fore-shadows the *reversion* of the office into a dream-world which is effected during the course of the action, as a place of hum-drum routine is gradually transmuted into a symbolic setting for Bill's estrangement, and the final curtain falls on the spiritual death of the hero.

The first scene's expository purposes are served partly by Bill's inarticulate attempt at a *curriculum vitae*. This duly reveals his name, his profession, and his employment of a managing-clerk called Hudson and of a junior called Jones—who turns out to be his own prosecuting counsel. But the dream also hints at Maitland's strong sexual appe-tite—he is arraigned on a charge of publishing and making known "a wicked, bawdy and scandalous object". [9] It suggests, too, his chronic hypochondria, and his excessive dependence on alcohol. All these personal traits are clus-tered into an ironic verbal collage:

Please forgive me. I have rather a headache. Perhaps that's why I'm here now. I had too much to drink last night, that's just the simple truth of it. Well, when I say that, I mean not much more than I usually have. Most nights. But that's well, I do drink quite a lot. Quite a lot? Oh, anyway, I'm what you'd call a serious drinker. That's to say, I just don't mess about once I get going—when I do. When I do? I nearly always do. I can drink a whole bottle of whisky. Can't be any good for the heart, can it? It must be a strain, pumping all that fire and damned rigour and everything all out again? Still, I'm pretty strong. I must be. Otherwise, I couldn't take it. That is, if I *can* take it. I can't, I'm sorry, I can't find my pills. I always have three or so in my ticket pocket. So sorry. [14–5]

This abrupt, egocentric, strongly associative idiom is typical of Bill—far more so than the Lucky-like speech which is his first contribution to the dream-proceedings, and which constitutes his substitute oath, a kind of creed of religio-technology, a statement of a belief he does not share in:

all the scientists who have ever lived in the history of the world since the days of Euclid, Pythagoras and Archimedes. Who, who are alive and at work today, today, now, at this time, in the inevitability of automation and the ever increasing need, need, oh, need for, the stable ties of modern family life, rethinking, reliving, making way for the motor car, forty million by nineteen; in a forward looking, outward looking, programme controlled machine tool line reassessment. With, yes, with faculties of memory and judgement far beyond the capacity of any human grief, being. Or any group of human who has ever lived. [10–1]

This is Maitland caught up in the mechanics of a half-understood jargon, verbalising those anti-values to which he is unable to conform—but which he is unable ultimately to reject. Because, as he admits in the office-courtroom, he is "to start with, and potentially and finally, that is to say, irredeemably mediocre". [17]

Maitland's speech-flow is often diverted into little rivulets of hatred against the symptoms of admass civilisation—its nourishment upon noise, its worship of the internal-combustion engine, its computerised thinking, its "slabs of concrete technological nougat", [30] its trivialisation of culture into colour-supplement fodder. It is directed, too, against the "flatulent, purblind, mating weasels" [24] such a society breeds:

> They: are the people who go up every year like it was holy communion to have a look at the Christmas decorations in Regent Street. They're the ones who drive the family fifty miles into the countryside and then park their cars beside the main road with a few dozen others, get out their thermos flasks, camp stools and primuses and do you know what they do? They sit and watch the long distance lorry drivers rattling past, and old people's coaches and all the other idiots like themselves about to do the same thing. [25]

There is, of course, nothing original about these antipathies, nor about the sense of estrangement from society that they induce. It is the frustrated energy of the hatred which makes them Maitland's own: and this "fibbing, mumping, pinched little worm of energy" [105–6] is constantly distorting itself into verbal grimaces against a society which is in the process of discarding him. Moreover, Maitland knows it: his tragedy is one of complete self-awareness. It is this *consciousness* of impotence in the face of destruction—a consciousness of energy turning in upon itself—which makes it possible for Osborne to reduce the roles of his minor characters to those of impressionistic pawns on the periphery of Maitland's personal endgame.

He exists for himself, however, only so long as he remains

an object in the existence of others: and when he ceases to sense this objectivity, it is time to sit back and await the end. He confesses in his dream-trial:

> I have always expected this, and, consequently, I have done my best to prepare myself as well as I can. [16]

But the preparation, as his inarticulate defence in the dream foreshadows, has been insufficient. And so, for the remainder of the first act, we witness Maitland's failure working itself out in the "real" day-to-day routines of a solicitor's office, routines on whose reality he still retains a kind of grip. But the second act assumes an increasingly impressionistic tone, in consonance with Maitland's loss of objective touch. Its occasional episodes of relative realism are not included arbitrarily or externally, but as intervals of lucidity during the progress of his breakdown.

It is impossible to underestimate the importance of *Inadmissible Evidence* having assumed such a solipsistic shape. It could so easily have become an *Epitaph for Bill Maitland*, carrying on in the kind of unpromising vein it strikes briefly in the aftermath of Bill's dream:

> HUDSON: Parky this morning.
> JONES: Yes.
> HUDSON: What's the matter then? Late night?
> JONES: No, not specially.
> HUDSON: How's that girl of yours?
> JONES: O.K.
> HUDSON: Still getting married?
> JONES: Suppose so. Got to get these finals out of the way first. Hardly see her except on Sundays. [21]

This is Osborne at his worst—striving for banality, and getting in an unnecessary bit of exposition to boot, but doing so in dialogue which fails even to be convincingly trivial. Significantly, the above banter occurs on the one and only occasion in the whole play when Maitland himself is off stage: he enters shortly afterwards, and there are few further lapses of style.

The play quickly sets about shedding some cold daylight on the character it has previously enmeshed in the blur of dream—a man who has already professed himself incapable of making decisions, regretful of those he has made, and, of course, "irredeemably mediocre". It is this Maitland who has confessed to "inflicting, quite certainly inflicting, more pain than pleasure" [20] in his sexual relationships, and who fears, above all else, "being found out" [19]—not only for "cooking up evidence on occasion or risking collusive agreements", [26] but for some deeper, more personal incapacity, some gigantic confidence trick which his very existence seems to be perpetrating on his fellow mortals. And increasingly this sense of incapacity has come to control his experience of reality:

However, however, my lord. I seem to retain very little. Very little indeed, hardly anything at all, in fact. Which is disturbing. Because I don't see how I can carry on my work even, well I am carrying on with it, but I must be getting less and less any good at it. *Even* my work, that's almost the least of it, which is probably, no doubt, one of the reasons I find myself here. . . . [18]

The failure foreshadowed in this passage assumes two complementary aspects during the course of the action—a personal failure to retain a sense of his own existence, and an eventually total failure to retain a sense of reciprocity in any of his human relationships.

Family, friends and business acquaintances fall away

from Bill like autumnal leaves from a tree—an inexorable process which has begun even before the play opens. His parents-in-law, for example, have long ceased to acknowledge his existence [103] and his wife exists only as an unheard voice—unheard, at least, by the audience. She may or may not be at the other end of a telephone line. And on the very evening before his dream, Maitland's visit with her to a dinner party has been marked by his feeling of being denied independent experience or existence. As he tells his mistress, Liz—again on the telephone, the medium through which Bill tries to retain a tenuous relationship with the outside world:

> I'm sorry. I just don't seem able to retain very much of anything, of anything that happened. . . . I just felt everyone was cutting me . . . cutting me . . . I know, I should care! I like them as much as they like me. . . . I don't know whether they're more afraid than I am. . . . I think they really *want* to be liked . . . in that sort of way. . . . I don't exactly do my best do I. No, well then. . . . No, Anna quite enjoyed herself while she was there. . . . Oh, the usual shower. . . . They all seem to adore her . . . I know, but more than ever . . . it's only all right when I'm with her. . . . Yes. . . . But it seemed at my expense this time, it seemed to be out of me . . . as if they were disowning me. . . . [52–3]

The morning on which the "real" action begins is marked by further failures to assert his own presence. These are carefully but not too obtrusively pointed. Maitland can't so much as hire a taxi, or get a good morning from the caretaker:

BILL: Things seem a bit odd. I still can't understand why

I couldn't get a taxi. They all had their lights on: for hire.
HUDSON: Well, you know what they are.
BILL: Yes, but I've never known it to happen to me before. Not in the morning.
HUDSON: You look all right. But if you'd like to. . . .
BILL: And the caretaker turned his back on me. I was walking up to the stairs and I was going to ask him—you know, quite politely—why the lift wasn't working. And he turned his back on me. [28]

These are early symptoms of an alienation that soon become acute. Shirley, Maitland's secretary and once one of his casual mistresses, has left by the end of the first act, and Hudson foreshadows his departure early in the second—for a rival firm.

What is important dramatically is not that an imposed pattern of desertions begins to emerge, but that it does so within a formal framework that can contain what would be —naturalistically—merely an over-convenient catalogue of coincidences. Not that the unfolding dramatic action lacks a *psychological* chain of causality. Its stylistic modulations, in short, develop Bill's gradually receding sense of reality in the first act into a total incapacity for objective relationships in the second. In this sense, *Inadmissible Evidence* can be regarded as spanning not so much the events of two successive days as the impressionistic, extra-temporal course of a nervous breakdown.

This, perhaps, savours overmuch of the kind of trimmed-off explanation detested by Osborne. But the dramatist himself defines the requisite change of style, in introducing the telephone conversation with Maitland's mistress which opens the second act:

This telephone conversation and the ones that follow it,

and some of the duologues should progressively resemble the feeling of dream and unreality of Bill's giving "evidence" at the beginning of Act 1. Some of the time it should all seem actually taking place at the particular moment, naturally, casual, lucid, unclouded. At others the grip of the dream grows tighter; for example, in the call that follows now, the presence of the person on the other end should be made very real indeed, but, sometimes it should trail off into a feeling of doubt as to whether there is anyone to speak to at all. [59]

Maitland is becoming increasingly aware of his need to exist for others in order to retain a hold on his own identity. Thus, of his wife, it was

> as if I only existed because of her, because she allowed me to, but if she turned off the switch . . . turned off the switch . . . who knows? But if she'd turned it off I'd have been dead. [62]

And the telephone conversations which take up so much of the second act convey something of this dramatically objectified solipsism. Formally, of course, they do so in a manner which much more readily suggests self-sufficiency than do the live duologues—into which a limited though diminishing reciprocity inevitably intrudes. The telephone becomes for Bill at once a means of and a symbol for contact with humanity. Osborne directs that it should be "stalked, abused, taken for granted, feared": and the worst fear is that of "being cut off", of no sound from the other end. [63]

But Osborne does not let this mechanical means of making his point do more than counterpoint Maitland's diminishing sense of direct human contact, which is theatrically much more difficult to convey. The telephone conversations thus

E

prepare the ground, metaphysically and stylistically, for the series of personal interviews which follow. These are with a succession of male and female clients—each played by the same actor or actress. One of the clients, Mrs Garnsey, has already been disposed of during the first act, at a time when Maitland, though distracted, was still in objective control. Even so, the problems of his client's husband turn out to be distressingly similar to his own:

> He comes home to me, and I know that nothing really works for him. Not at the office, not his friends, not even his girls. I wish they would. God knows, he tries hard enough. I wish I could help him. But I can't, and everyone, everyone, wherever, we go together, whether it's a night out, or an evening at our club, or an outing with the children, everyone's, I know, everyone's drawing away from him. And the more people have been good and kind and thoughtful to me, the worse it's been for him. I know. And now. Now: *I'm* doing the same thing. The children hardly notice him. And now it's *me*. I can't bear to see him rejected and laughed at and scorned behind his back and ignored. . . . [55]

We never meet Anna, Bill's own wife. There is no need: this could very well be her own description of her husband's estrangement. Such an overlapping of dramatic functions attunes us to the role of the clients in the second act—most of whom are similarly embodiments of certain reactions *towards* Maitland, and not "real" individuals in need of his professional help.

After Mrs Garnsey's departure, Maitland has to call in his telephonist, Joy, simply in order to reassure himself of his reality. This he can only now do by seducing her: but "nothing really works for him . . . not even his girls". In the second act we learn that Mrs Garnsey has been scared off. "In some way", Maitland admits, "I could feel her withdrawing from me." [76] But the day's first visitors, Mrs Tonks and Mrs Anderson, are both played by the same actress as Mrs Garnsey. Signifiying what? A second and a third chance of retaining contact—both lost? The sameness of all Maitland's relationships with his women? The symbolic fragmentation of his breakdown? Or a simple matter of economy in casting? There is no ready or self-sufficient answer, for Osborne has inextricably blended his technical and thematic requirements so that each reinforces the other.

The subsequent appearance of a Mr Maples—played by the actor who has previously taken the part of Jones—confirms that the importance of the clients lies not only in the cumulative force of their successive desertions, but in their functions as mirrors of Maitland's own situation. Mrs Garnsey stands in for any one of Bill's women, wanting yet unable to love him, because of his compulsive need to withdraw—as he eventually does both from his wife and his current mistress. Mrs Tonks is any one of the women who respond to him—or to his "excessive sexual appetite", as she more accurately puts it, ostensibly of her own husband [78] —in purely physical terms, and who move on, hurt or bored, as Shirley has done and as Joy is about to do. And Mrs Anderson and Maples are distorted images of Maitland himself: for the focus of his isolation is narrowing, and even the style of the dialogue in these later "interviews" is introspective rather than communicative.

Maples, however, is a homosexual—it is this that has got him into trouble with the law. Thus, his story is not only one of increasing isolation, but of a life constantly prepared for the inevitable confrontation with a plain-clothes policeman in the Piccadilly Circus lavatories—just as Bill has "always expected" the final account he is now rendering.

Maples, too, leaves—for good, like the other clients. Jane, Bill's daughter, arrives—and departs. "You'll go out of that door and I'll not see you again," he tells her, "I am quite sure of *that* by this time if nothing else." [105] The certainty is justified. Hudson and Jones have also left, and Joy decides to take the next day off—and no doubt the days after it as well. Only Liz remains. But as Maitland has promised earlier, she "may be the last to pack it in, but pack it in she will" [64]—and, confounded by her lover's total inability to be helped, the "last to pack it in" she proves to be. Maitland has now only to cut himself off from his wife— finally to "put the receiver down" on a relationship that has existed for the audience only in telephonic terms—and to await the summons of the Law Society . . . or whatever. [115]

This is the most dominant of several thematic strands which can be traced through the play. I have separated it out not to produce a pat analysis of the action—though its progress towards Maitland's total isolation is explicated in the dialogue too insistently to be accidental—but in order to demonstrate the certainty with which the play's dramatic development matches its formal movement, which slowly reverts from documentary realism to the impressionism fore- shadowed in the play's nightmare prologue. But the investi- gation of Maitland's character—and the investigation of Maitland's character *is* the play—is far more complex than my concentration on its final progress towards breakdown might suggest. Indeed, that progress could scarcely have been more than mechanical unless Maitland's personality were seen to have been *formed* by a far fuller body of experi- ences and emotions than those to which it is eventually nar- rowed down. And Maitland is, indeed, made to live not just in his immediate disintegration, but in his ironic or regretful awareness of what he might have been. Here, of course, Osborne is on familiar ground, for Maitland is constantly looking back in nostalgia—just as he is seeking in the future a security he now knows it cannot contain.

No doubt Maples is echoing Maitland's own sentiments—as indeed he might be echoing those of Jimmy Porter and Alison—in his feeling that "being young" never happened to him. [93] Certainly, Maitland himself loves and hates youth with an intensity brought into sharpest focus in the long, soliloquising tirade against his daughter, Jane. It would, perhaps, have been better to modify the presentation of this soliloquy so that it took place at Bill's end of his telephone line. Though the change of stylistic gear is prepared for by an emphatic fade, [101] the mute physicality of Jane's presence on stage doesn't quite predicate the image that was presumably intended: of Jane ignoring Maitland in her turn—just as Mrs Garnsey's children "hardly notice" their father—and of Maitland, in this, his final "interview", reduced to the one-way communication of his monologue.

But the soliloquy does encapsulate a middle-ageing jealousy-cum-contempt for the young that is vintage Osborne:

> Oh, I read about you, I see you in the streets. I hear what you say, the sounds you make, the few jokes you make, the wounds you inflict without even longing to hurt, there is no lather or fear in you, all cool, dreamy, young, cool and not a proper blemish, forthright, unimpressed, contemptuous of ambition but good and pushy all the same. You've no shame of what you are, and, very little, well, not much doubt as to what you'll become. [104]

And consider the self-revelation and the social comment which combine here into an indictment of the cult of coolness:

You are unselfconscious, which I am not. You are without guilt, which I am not. Quite rightly. Of course, you are stuffed full of paltry relief for emergent countries, and marches and boycotts and rallies, you, you kink your innocent way along tirelessly to all that poetry and end- less jazz and folk worship, *and* looking gay and touching and stylish all at the same time. But there isn't much loving in any of your kindnesses, Jane, not much kindness, not even cruelty, really, in any of you, not much craving for the harm of others, perhaps just a very easy, con- trolled sharp, I mean "sharp" pleasure in discomfiture. [106]

The strings of simple connectives and the successive qualifica- tions which reduce "style" to "sharpness" ensure that the passage develops at once rhetorically and logically. It's notable how much more successful it is in defining Maitland's idea of "youth" than the attempted physical embodiment of that idea in the well-bedded Joy:

JOY: The draught under that door's a bit much, though. And it was a bit of a shock opening the door to your old woman.
BILL: But you don't regret it?
JOY: Maybe there'll be other times, other places. And if not, well. . . . [71]

This shows up clearly the limits of Osborne's verbal empathy, and is flawed by much the same unsubtle use of jargon and supposed youthful commonplace as is his later portrayal of the despised younger sister in *Time Present*. "There'll be other times, other places," indeed! Not that there are, of course: and that Joy's departure is alone in failing to seem inevitable, alone in seeming no more than a dramatic necessity, is symptomatic of Osborne's uncertainty about her character. He is similarly uncertain about Jane's character, though the nature of its stylisation is of his own choosing—just as he is less convincing in drawing what he calls the "puny arrogance and closed mind" [91] of Jones, who is cast in much the same mould as Graham Dodd in *The Entertainer*, than he is with the phlegmatic, comfortable and broadly sympathetic Hudson.

But the play isn't really about these other characters, still less is it objectively about "youth". It is, in part, about Bill Maitland's feelings *towards* youth, and these Osborne can render as subtly elsewhere as he does with the stops out in Maitland's indictment of Jane. Even this indictment, however, pauses for a few moments of nostalgia—a nostalgia that is now no more than wish-fulfilment:

> I always used to think . . . that when you're the age you are now, I'd take you out to restaurants for dinner, big restaurants like I used to think posh restaurants were like, with marble columns and glass and orchestras. Like Lyons used to be before you knew it. And I thought we'd behave like a rather grand married couple, a bit casual but with lots and lots of signals for one another. And waves of waiters would pass in front of us and admire us and envy us and we'd dance together. . . . Very slowly. [102]

Now compare this passage with Maitland's earlier daydream of regaining his lost independence—a loneliness that might be, as it were, chosen and dignified, not imposed upon him unwillingly:

> There was a time when I used to speculate about *her* death. Oh, but not only Anna's. I'd be crunching back up that new path with the planks and the wet clay and

the flowers. Perhaps I'd have walked out of that place on my own, there'd have been no one else, I could have done as I liked. I could have sat in Lyons and got myself a cup of coffee and a roll and butter all on my own. I might have looked around me, and my throat would have been tight and I'd have trouble with my coffee, and I'd smile sentimentally at the coloured girl who was clearing away the plates just because she was coloured, and my throat seemed to be closed up with the business of dying, and I'd kid myself we were friendly to one another. [86]

Both these speeches capture exactly the quality of Maitland's nostalgia—slightly down-at-heel and old-fashioned, highly analytical of the actual sensations of pleasure and of independence, and hopeful of recapturing an art of casual communication he has long since lost.

But the direction of events into such chosen courses is now beyond Maitland's control:

I want to feel tender, I want to be comforting and encouraging and full of fun and future things and things like that. But all I feel is as if my head were bigger and bigger, spiked and falling off, like a mace, it gets in my way, or keeps getting too close. [35]

This is the Maitland of the first act, conscious of his malaise, but uncertain of its nature—who keeps trying to "enjoy things, enjoy other people . . . and the circle just seems to get smaller". [33] This is the Maitland who gradually retreats into the world of his own nightmare, a place where an account is demanded of him but cannot be rendered:

I don't have any idea where I am. I have tried not to cause pain, I really have, you think I haven't, but I do try, I ought to be able to give a better account of myself. But I don't seem to be functioning properly. I don't seem to retain anything, at least not for very long. I wish I could go back to the beginning, except I wouldn't do any better. [40]

"Gradually being deserted and isolated," as he later describes himself to Maples, Maitland can "grasp so little, trust nothing," and cannot be "expected to be capable of giving a decent account" of himself. [92] This recurrent image of rendering an account—like such other motifs as the Lyons restaurants—are integral to the process of his characterisation: and they simultaneously give definition to the narrowing boundaries of his world. What is remarkable is that Osborne can create at one stroke an impression of this gradual whittling-away of experience—and of the complex personality which has emerged thus atrophied from the emotional battlefields of two decades of adulthood.

I referred to the action earlier as Maitland's endgame: and *Inadmissible Evidence* is truly the most Beckettian of Osborne's plays in the remorselessness of its movement and the economy of its means. Yet its associations with a chess-game have to do with more than a literary metaphor. Maitland, like the king on the chessboard, is the only figure who ultimately matters, yet he has little capacity for acting in his own defence. He is dependent on the interaction of forces around him: but in this game the only remaining pawns are of the opposition, and, like Shirley, "conspiring to kill me". [49]

In the dramatic metaphor which hems in Maitland's life, however, the conspiracy is not one of siege but of abandonment. In "real life", of course, the next morning and the charladies would arrive long before the Law Society—which is why *Inadmissible Evidence* does depend, more than any other of Osborne's plays, upon being interpreted metaphorically if it is to achieve self-consistency. A possible interpretation I have offered. And one thing at least is certain. Once every other character but Maitland himself has finally departed into the wings, only the fall of the curtain is possible: and it falls, however one cares to juggle with the terms of a chosen metaphor, not just on a day but on a life.

9

A Patriot for Me

A PATRIOT FOR ME is, like *Luther*, an exploration of a persisting human problem within a particular historical period. The problem is that of the assimilation of the homosexual into his society, and its period is the decadence of the Austro-Hungarian Empire. The action spans twenty-three years in time, requiring almost as many mutually distinct scene-changes—and these need to be more closely realistic than those of *Slickey* or *Luther*, the only other of Osborne's stage plays for which he has specified more than a single or adaptable setting.

A Patriot for Me[26] is a technically ambitious and experimental piece: and as an experiment it was worth making, though its success is incomplete. After the one-man-stand that was *Inadmissible Evidence*, Osborne here attempted to control his largest-ever cast. And as a result—cursory though the glimpses of most of its thirty-odd identified members are—the play's central character, Alfred Redl, is more believably caught up in a broad social complex than any of Osborne's earlier heroes. And this is appropriate, since Redl makes a more persistent effort to compromise his own exceptional identity, at least than any of his predecessors. His failure is one of self-awareness, and its consequences are tragic.

The action of *A Patriot for Me* takes place mainly in the higher military echelons of Arthur Schnitzler's Vienna, into which Alfred Redl has forced a determined way, overcoming an insignificant birth by a combination of tact and hard work—attributes for which few earlier Osborne heroes are particularly remarkable. But Redl's career is similar in two senses to that of his creator's other historical characters, Holyoake and Luther. It has its roots in reality:[27] and its hero sows the seeds of his own estrangement. The historical Redl was estranged both as a homosexual and a Jew: but his Jewishness does not particularly concern Osborne, and it is revealed (almost incidentally) only in the penultimate scene of the play. [126]

Indeed, it is not till the climax of the first of the play's three acts that Redl is even aware of himself as a homo-sexual—and Osborne seems pedantically determined that his audience's awareness shall be similarly slow to develop. In fact, the play's censorship troubles—it was eventually mounted as a club-production outside the Lord Chamber-lain's jurisdiction, at the Royal Court Theatre in June 1965—ensured that its theme was notorious long before the curtain rose on its first night, and the function of suspense was fortuitously but fortunately minimised. For like all dramatic literature which claims more than topical or ephemeral interest, A Patriot for Me has to succeed at a second, third or fourth sitting, not only at a single acquaint-ance: and the sensed irony of the audience's foreknowledge was in the event a more valuable adjunct to the play's early scenes than any exercise in sexual trait-trapping might have been. But Osborne nevertheless indulges in some heavily-pointed teasing. As a result, Redl's first scene—in which he acts as duelling second to a young man who has been dubbed Fräulein Rothschild by his victorious antagonist—strikes one rather as an opening clue in a guessing game than as a piece in a psychological jigsaw-puzzle to which the audience already has the key.

Various further clues are planted. Redl cries in his sleep during an abortive affair with a countess—who begins

wooing him in her line of duty as an intelligence agent, but
falls in love with him in the process. He admits that such
spasms occur:

> Just at a bad time. In the night. Or when I'm having to
> force myself to do something as an exercise, or a duty, like
> working late. [58]

Or, of course, like forcing himself to sleep with a woman,
instead of the man he subconsciously desires—as he desired
the effeminately handsome young duellist of the first scene.
He is unable to "bring himself to dismiss" an obliging waiter,
[30] in order to attend the whore to whom a friend offers to
treat him—and in whose arms he almost faints. [35] Finally,
a fellow customer solicits him in a café, and responds to a
curt dismissal by saying softly, "I know what *you're* looking
for." [67]

Redl, we are informed, looks stricken. And Osborne
evidently wants his audience to share the trauma. Quite
apart from its impracticability once the play is known and
being talked about, this desire to indulge in a process of
psychological titillation—which culminates in Redl's
moment of self-discovery—unbalances Osborne's first act;
because *A Patriot for Me* is not impressionistic, like *Inadmissible Evidence*: and it is in other respects distinguished by a
formal *objectivity* towards its central character which is rarely
found in the earlier plays. And this objectivity demands an
appropriately cerebral awareness from an audience.

A similar tendency to tricksiness is apparent at the beginning of the drag-ball in the second act. Here Osborne directs
that the operatic duet with which the act opens should "be
accepted at the beginning as the indifferent effort of a court
opera house cast with amateurs", [71] and not as the
transvestite prank it really is. Such sexual obtuseness serves

no apparent purpose. The ambiguity can in any case only come off once—and Osborne's declaration in the same scene that it "is essential that it should only gradually be revealed to the audience that all the dancers and guests are men" is equally inexplicable. [72] *Why* is it essential—unless as an in-joke or a production gimmick?

The guests themselves are in no doubt as to their sex or their sexuality, and no longer, even, is Alfred Redl. It is, then, both disruptive and distracting to try to keep the secret from an audience which has already been over-carefully clued-in to Redl's condition. The suddenness of his self-discovery has already tended to reflect on his own credibility: and now, instead of allowing his audience to observe a fascinating transvestite occasion on its own terms, Osborne makes a further attempt to mislead. That the attempt cannot work more than once only adds the charge of technical maladroitness to that of insulting the spectator's intelligence. The clue-dropping process is, admittedly, irritating rather than fatally disruptive: it is simply a pity that Osborne felt it to be necessary at all.

The graph of *Patriot's* plot-construction follows a traditional curve. The first act is concerned with Redl's progress towards self-awareness, the second with his brief attempt at self-realisation, and the third with his self-destruction. These natural stages are not, in the event, too perfectly segmented for probability: rather, they give to the play's two intervals a punctuating purpose they now seldom serve. And that Redl's eventual death—an honourable suicide chosen in preference to a treason trial for betraying his country's secrets under pressure of blackmail—is accomplished almost too theatrically is a matter of history rather than dramatic choice. Though one does, perhaps, get the feeling that history has moments too melodramatic to be successfully translated into "realistic" theatre!

At least, realistic the play aspires to be. Only towards the very end does Redl's tongue sometimes run away with him in the manner of the verbally introverted Osborne heroes—significantly, at moments of sexual tension. [117–19] Previously, he has been a model of rhetorical restraint—the first of Osborne's central characters to be realised as much through what he does as what he says. He does not often *talk at* his companions: he tries, often tortuously, to use words for the interchange of ideas and emotions. But the interchange is seldom more than tactical, and ultimately Redl succeeds no better in establishing verbal or any other kind of human reciprocity than George Dillon, Jimmy Porter or Bill Maitland.

It is, presumably, implicit in Osborne's attitude towards homosexuality that it is not, in itself, either unusual or exceptionable. His homosexual hero has therefore to submit to suffering an "exceptional" isolation among his own sexual kind. But the necessity to mark out Redl's loneliness involves Osborne in further dramatically incongruous situations. Thus the drag ball is a brilliant *coup de théâtre*: but it is the kind of affair that only the most flamboyant of homosexuals would be likely to attend. And although Redl's eventual disgusted exit does cut him off from such elements in his chosen society, it is unlikely that the Redl of the earlier scenes would have been tempted into flaunting his proclivities in such a manner—though this may be only another instance of Osborne's tendency to indulge in instantaneous developments of character, the causes of which he is reluctant to explore.

Certainly, the emphatic-interval allows him to *assume* the period of Redl's immediate coming-to-terms with his condition: and Osborne, in the event, seems more concerned to use the ball itself for documentary than for dramatic purposes. He even interpolates a lengthy note on drag convention into his printed text, [73–4] and his concern for verisimilitude makes for intriguing theatre—but this very theatricality sore-thumbs its lengthy way into the more restrained episodes which add up to the rest of the play. A lot of unnecessary explanation is written into the text of the scene—ostensibly for the initiate Redl's benefit—concerning the organisation and ethics of the ball, and some of this is of the most obtrusive kind:

BARON: What fun! I do enjoy these things. I wish we could have one every month. I'm so glad you liked Ferdy.
KUNZ: How long is it now?
BARON: Three years.
KUNZ: Long time.
BARON: For me. Let's be honest, for nearly all of us. [81]

This verges between dramatically justifiable self-pity and sociology. And at other moments the dialogue descends into the idiom of propagandist oratory:

We are none of us safe. This . . . is the celebration of the individual against the rest, the us's and the them's, the free and the constricted, the gay and the dreary, the lonely and the mob, the little Tsarina there and the Emperor Francis Joseph. [77]

All the scene adds to our knowledge of Redl is that he is *not* cut out for the kind of orgiastic homosexuality celebrated in such a speech. It does also hint that his fellow-guests put down his military prowess to an attempt at sexual sublimation, of the cold-bath variety:

Tried everything, apparently. Resolutions, vows, religion, medical advice, self-exhaustion. Used to flog a dozen horses into the ground in a day. And then gardening, if you please, fencing and all those studies they do, you do, of course—military history, ciphers, telegraphy, campaigns, he knows, hundreds of them, by heart. He knows his German literature, speaks superb French and Russian, Italian, Polish, Czech *and* Turkish if you please. [82–3]

But no sublimation theory is put to a theatrical test in the portrayal of Redl, so that its proposition here makes for an arbitrary complication. We witness Redl flirting with the bum-boys—which involves a quick-change of character, attributed to the dramatically-convenient effects of drink—and then reverting to taciturn form, striking one of them to the ground, and departing. [91] It makes a good curtain to a strong scene: and it is a basic weakness of *A Patriot for Me* that one is thus reduced to discussing it in isolatively "theatrical" terms, and not in terms appropriate to an insightful examination of a particular human being and a particular sexual condition.

Osborne has, in short, been altogether more careful about his effects than about his effect. Elsewhere, he makes an amusing reference to Redl's seduction of an English schoolboy, whose Etonian boater graces his bedroom as a souvenir: [84] and then he retrospectively sours the anecdotal impression by getting Redl's blackmailers to produce the boater as incriminating evidence from a paper bag. [98] What had seemed simply *true* was no more than a Scribean clue.

But if incidents add up too neatly, characters sometimes don't add up at all. It was the critic of *The Times* who commented after the play's first production that Osborne's feelings about the individual and society had not yet "found a common focus". And the feeling of a play working on two dissociated levels does pervade *A Patriot for Me*. It is (an unfamiliar criticism to be levelling at Osborne) *too* objective to permit the kind of insights into the workings of Redl's mind that are, for example, gained into Bill Maitland's. Military society is served up in episodic snippets: and Redl is, in fact, dramatically most successful as link-man to a whole host of bit-players. His personal tragedy, however, is essentially one of inability to adjust to that society: and his objective and subjective roles in consequence tend to collide.

Redl's life is conceived very much as a sequence of failures. He suffers sexual failures in encounters with whores and mistresses, successively of the female and the male variety, and social failures in adapting to the military *élite* into which he has worked his way. And, strangely, Osborne is much more successful in conveying an impression of this *élite* than he is in setting Redl at odds with it. This success varies, indeed, in something like an inverse proportion to the amount of light a scene is intended to throw on Redl's condition.

There is, for example, the episode set in a lecture theatre, in which the analyst Schoepfer discourses on the mental causes of homosexuality. [92] Schoepfer is put on display somewhat dissonantly, as a caricature who is humorously obsessed—in the Jonsonian sense—with his subject. But this matters less than the failure of his lecture—and of its climactic counterpart, [127] in which it transpires, rather puzzlingly, that he is next on the list for screening as a potential spy—to throw ironical light upon the characters who are rendered in human terms as homosexuals. All Osborne is doing, it seems, is getting in a casual hit at those who have a reach-me-down "cure" for homosexuality—this, in a play which is not so much about a homosexual among heterosexuals, as about one who fails even among his own kind.

In this respect, the scene in a mental hospital, in which

Redl visits one of his former boy-friends—now both married and mad—ought to be strikingly relevant, but is actually somewhat baffling. It concludes with this exchange:

> REDL: Mischa, do you know where you are?
> MISCHA: On a star, sir, on a star. Just like you. I expect you were sent to Vienna too, sir, because you are the same kind of element as me The same dual body functioning. [111]

Dual body functioning, forsooth! Whatever purpose the scene serves, its wisdom-in-madness is no less trite or pretentious than Schoepfer's psychologising. And it is a mark of how inappropriately externalised Osborne's technique becomes that Redl's final choice—between standing trial as a spy and accepting his chance of suicide—assumes interest only as an old-fashioned matter of military honour:

> MÖHL: How people will enjoy this, they'll enjoy this. The *élite* caught out! Right at the centre of the Empire. You know what they'll say, of course? About the *élite*.
> TAUSSIG: Perhaps it can be kept a secret, sir. Do you think? It's still possible.
> MÖHL: Yes. We must do it now. Where is Redl? [121]

This caricatures itself: yet it must be assumed that this is the issue as Möhl and Taussig present it to Redl, and that it is on such a ground that he does indeed determine to commit suicide—for no other influences are made dramatically operative. Moreover, the scene in which Redl makes up his mind offstage—as three muffled men wait in the street for the sound of the fatal shot—heightens the impression that he has, indeed, chosen an "honourable" suicide, at a moment when irony seems most requisite. [124] There *is* climactic irony, but this relates to the political, not the personal level of the play. A penultimate scene thus returns to the documentary manner which evokes imperial decadence so well in the earlier social episodes: and a parliamentary debate about Redl's suicide—which could not be hushed up, after all—drones along its scandalised way convincingly enough. [125–6] But Redl as an individual has disappeared long before his death, as the play's focus shifts from his private struggle to its "public" plot.

Perhaps this will prove to be the importance of *A Patriot for Me* in a fuller retrospect—that it enabled Osborne to broaden his techniques of peripheral characterisation and of etching in the contours of a social environment. Redl's countess says of the imperial army that it provides "a context of expression for people, who wouldn't otherwise have it". [49] And Osborne has rendered this context with admirable economy—as in no other of his earlier plays, with the possible and rather special exception of *The Entertainer*. Later, the titular setting of *Hotel in Amsterdam* was to serve a similar purpose rather more organically: for in *A Patriot for Me*, the contextualising *alternates* with the definition of Redl's isolation, instead of complementing it. Kunz suggests a possible means by which a fusion of the two techniques might have been tempered theatrically and historically:

> We all play parts, *are* doing so now, *will* continue to do so, and as long as we are playing at being Austrian, Viennese, or whatever we think we are, cosmopolitan and nondescript, a position palmed on us by history, by the accident of having held back the Muslim horde at the gates of Europe. [49]

It could have been Redl's inability to adopt such a "role" in the military *élite* which condemned him to isolation and to discovery: such an explanation, however glib, would at least have given the social and personal forces at work in the play a common focus. But this is to extrapolate, not to criticise.

Perhaps it is no coincidence that Osborne's most successful attempt at *socialising* his art did occur in *A Patriot for Me*— since it is the closest he has ever come to dealing in dramatic terms with that era of certainty before the first world war which has so consistently and incongruously attracted him. Perhaps, at least, his sympathies for Alison's father, for Billy Rice, for the unseen Gideon Orme in *Time Present*—and even for Lord Mortlake—help to explain the sureness of touch with which he has sketched in Redl's kindly superiors, Möhl and Hötzendorf, and their world of confidences-over-brandy and of parties at the Hofburg. *A Patriot for Me* remains a challenging and ambitious work, in which Osborne made a tentative advance towards new formal frontiers, but failed to hold some of his more familiar territory.

10

A Bond Honoured

A BOND HONOURED is an adaptation of Lope de Vega's
La Fianza Satisfecha. Only in Osborne's choice of title is his
actual *translation* of the work more accurate than the version
previously available in English—buried in a back number
of the *Tulane Drama Review*, and there dubbed *The Outrageous
Saint*.[28] But as Osborne's note to his printed text makes plain,
it was never his intention to recreate Lope's play either in
letter or in spirit:

> In 1963, Kenneth Tynan, Literary Manager of the
> National Theatre, asked me if I would adapt *La Fianza
> Satisfecha* by Lope de Vega. It was in three acts, had an
> absurd plot, some ridiculous characters and some very
> heavy humour. What did interest me was the Christian
> framework of the play and the potentially fascinating
> dialectic with the principal character. So I concentrated
> on his development (in the original he rapes his sister in
> the opening moments of the play without any preparatory
> explanation of his character or circumstances) and dis-
> carded most of the rest, reducing the play to one long
> act. *A Bond Honoured* is the result. [9]

It was duly produced at the National Theatre in June 1966,
in unlikely harness with Peter Shaffer's *Black Comedy*—a piece
originally conceived as a makeweight to *Miss Julie*, and
which was to outlast Osborne as it had outrun Strindberg.
Not since *The World of Paul Slickey*, in fact, was a play by

Osborne received with such universal disapprobation: though whether the fault lay with Lope or with his adapter most reviewers, not having read the original, weren't very clear. Osborne's note suggests that it would be unfair to assess *A Bond Honoured* in too close correlation with its original, and it might, indeed, be kindest to the dramatist to ignore *La Fianza Satisfecha* altogether: for it proves, upon investigation, to be by far the better play of the two. But this is one of the things that makes a comparison so illuminating: for it is in this kind of free adaptation that one has the best chance of observing the artist's prerogative of *selectivity* in operation. Instead of shaping a work of art from his own imagination and experience—into which it would be impertinent and usually impossible for the critic to probe— the dramatist in such a case has allowed an existing and generally available body of material to gestate in his mind. The play that is re-born in the process of rejection, of reshaping, and of applying a personalised dramatic overlay, reveals authorial intentions and preoccupations much more readily than the work which is entirely original in content: and, so long as the critic steers clear of the biographical fallacy, a constructive comparison between two "given" works is made possible.

In spite of Osborne's prefatory reference to his "one long act", his printed text separates the play into two parts, as opposed to Lope's three. But this inconsistency is unimportant, for both dramatists have chosen to shape dramatic entities out of a succession of episodes that lack much chronological or geographical unity. What does need taking up in Osborne's note is its slighting reference to the ingredients he has discarded from his original—its "absurd plot, some ridiculous characters and some very heavy humour". For most of these elements could be found in a large proportion of the plays of the renaissance now generally regarded as masterpieces. May not Osborne, then, be depriving his hero of a "ridiculous" background which is in fact vital if his dramatic existence is to be made viable? Lear, after all, can be no more adequately anatomised into latter-day dialectics than his daughters. Is it really any more feasible to concentrate, as Osborne wishes, on the "development" of Lope's Leonido—an embodiment of motiveless malignity—having "discarded" the conventions through which such a character lives?

Well, to some extent it might be—in Leonido's case, at least—by reshaping his character into the more fashionable form of a sexual hedonist, and by working out an existential framework to predicate his actions. Such a hedonist is what Osborne has started—but curiously enough *only* started—to make of Leonido: a regressive amoralist, who sets out to compensate for his own insufficiency by merging the fantasies of adolescence into his real-life relationships. Developing such a theme—the consequences of a failure to achieve reciprocity in human relationships—would have been a reworking of familiar territory for Osborne. But the territory his hero treads is that of the renaissance—both physically and metaphysically. Osborne's scenes, like Lope's, shift between an apparently lawless Sicily and an anarchic Tunis—enabling Leonido to indulge himself fully without much legal impediment. In this way, the setting becomes that never-never land of pornographia, where actions have no consequences and crimes no retribution.

Now there's no aesthetic or even moral reason why Osborne shouldn't have explored such a theme, or have chosen to do so by reworking a play that was actually about the Christian redemption which even such a vile sinner as Leonido might attain. In Lope's play, Leonido rapes his sister, assaults his father and brother-in-law, and turns Mohammedan in order to sully his family's blood. He then meets Christ, disguised as a shepherd—and subsequently in his own form—undergoes a pauline trauma of conversion, and finally triumphs "as one who has found his identity".[29] Now Osborne's Leonido also meets Christ: but he seeks retribution *without* repentance. Strangely, Lope's hero is of the New Testament, and Osborne's is of the Old. He pays with his life—which is "no more than fluff at the bottom of the pocket" [55]—for crimes in which he dies exulting.

To Leonido's atrocities as enumerated by Lope is added—purely for shock-value, it seems—the rape of his own mother. [59] This makes Marcela not only Leonido's sister and his mistress, but his daughter as well. The heaping of sexual horror upon horror is strangely similar to that which cast its unnecessarily dark shadow over Tim and Jenny in *Under Plain Cover*, in which fetishism was arbitrarily complicated by incest. And the trouble is that such excesses do not so much challenge an audience's sensibilities as suggest kinds of causality which are not to Osborne's purpose at all. Is it *because* they are brother and sister, one finds oneself asking, that Tim and Jenny in *Under Plain Cover* are also fetishists? Is it *because* he has raped his mother—who "hardly resisted" [38]—that Leonido in *A Bond Honoured* has become what he is? And is it *because* he is really her father that Marcela reciprocates his affection?

Lope was really much the subtler strategist in making Leonido's sins at once impulsively evil, and exclusively his own—as he was in not seeking to motivate them rationally, any more than Shakespeare can be said to "motivate" Iago, or Middleton to "motivate" De Flores in *The Changeling*. Osborne's incest-theme actually comes closer to resembling Ford's in *Tis Pity She's a Whore* than to Lope's. For in *La Fianza Satisfecha*, Marcela is repelled by her brother's attempted rape. And Leonido, incidentally, appears to derive sexual satisfaction from drawing his sister's blood after his rebuttal, as if from the thwarted rape itself—a point of some psychological insight. From such clues, in fact, a reasonably credible Freudian interpretation of Lope's play, which does involve masochistic suffering in expiation of sadistic guilt, can be worked out.[30] But the self-consistency of the piece makes such an exercise unnecessary and academic.

Ford achieves consistency of another kind. In *Tis Pity*, he has Annabella and Giovanni *share* their incestuous love: and the fates of both brother and sister are thus fulfilled within a single dramatic action. As this precedent suggests, the greater degree of Marcela's complicity in Osborne's version of Lope's play at once complicates Leonido's role as sadist, and creates a dramatic need for a more telling climax to Marcela's own part in the action. This need is particularly strong because Osborne has retained the gist of Lope's conclusion, which involves various setbacks and recognitions— and these assume the retention of his own stylised framework if they are to transcend the farcical. In short, Lope was working within conventions appropriate to his climax: but Leonido's lonely fulfilment in *A Bond Honoured* leaves Marcela, and the play itself, at a loose end.

Osborne has, however, retained Lope's assignment of the final tag to Tizon, Leonido's phlegmatic manservant:

Well, King, he played a good tune on vituperation. It may not be a bond honoured, but it's a tune of sorts to end with. [62]

Having cut most of the so-called "heavy humour" of the original—which in fact consists of some passably amusing and certainly leavening crosstalk between the manservant and his Moorish counterpart—it is odd that Osborne should allow Tizon the last word. Perhaps it is one of the few attempts the script makes to accommodate the self-conscious style of staging for which Osborne's opening direction calls:

> All the actors in the play sit immobile in a circle through-
> out most of the action. When those who are all in the
> same scene rise to take part in it, they all do so together.

Now this has the obvious effect of distancing the action. And
yet Osborne continues:

> The acting style is hard to discover or describe. I will just
> say: it must be extremely violent, pent-up, toppling on
> and over the edge of animal howlings and primitive rage.
> At the same time, it should have an easy, modern natural-
> ness, even in the most extravagant or absurd moments.
> [15]

The requirement seems to be for Artaudian tailoring of
stylistic lounge-suits: certainly it is at once more demanding
and less evidently purposeful than anything pertaining to
style previously specified by Osborne. But it is at least an
attempt at a convention able to contain the "absurd plot" he
has inherited—a plot which, paradoxically, he comes close
to endowing with "absurdity" of a more contemporary kind.
Conceived and consistently executed in terms of the ritualised
fantasy of a Jean Genet, Lope's theme might even have been
metamorphosed into a viable modern form. But Osborne,
in spite of his own directions, has failed to avoid his familiar
pitfall of over-explicitness: and the resultant *rationale* is too
top-heavy to sustain the ritual.

It is again the brother-sister relationship that causes the
trouble. Lope begins his play during Leonido's first attempt
to rape his sister, but Osborne carefully shocks us into awareness that the affair is of much longer standing. It is, Leonido
tells Tizon:

Three nights since I slept and then only for a few minutes before I was tipped out by my sister. [17]

Tizon takes up the hint by referring to what "may or may not in the past . . . have occurred between you and your sister". [18] And even the suggestion of a doubt here is quickly dispelled by Leonido:

Not may or may not have. Has. Did. Is. Not was, might, may. *Is*. Well? [18]

The incest, then, is of the past as well as the present. That it is also to be perpetuated in the future is soon established in Marcela's bedchamber, [23–5] and in Leonido's remarks to Tizon on the subject of a subsequent, interrupted visit. [31–2] Here, the first two lines are in Lope's play—but the third is Osborne's addition, which significantly modifies the implication of the exchange:

LEONIDO: It's done.
TIZON: But not well. Was it?
LEONIDO: No, not well this time, but let's say we celebrated all the occasions past when it *was* well done. [33]

In the original, Tizon's allusion was to a moral failure: here it is to a failure of sexual consummation. *A Bond Honoured* thus becomes not a "fascinating dialectic" about Christianity at all, but a play about a brother's jealous reaction to his sister's marriage—a marriage which, he asserts, is being made not for love but money. Leonido accuses his father, Gerardo, and his brother-in-law, Dionisio, of

Talking dowries and property and being important over my sister's body and disposing of it—as they think. [19]

And in the second scene in Marcela's bedchamber Leonido is made to avow:

It is only in you that I see a foot ahead of me and my heartbeat recovers. What is it now? A life of scavenging for slops of your attention. Eh? Upturned from the window to your bedchamber? Remember my mouth, my mouth, your mouth, Marcela. [32]

Of course, Leonido may not be telling the emotional truth. But it would be unlike him to assume anything less than frankness in his amorality, and both this scene and its earlier counterpart do develop a romantic affection between brother and sister which makes such a declaration consonant with Leonido's actions. The demotion of Dionisio, Marcela's husband, to a minor role—that of comic cuckolded husband, rather than injured man of honour—makes one's assurance of the depth of the relationship doubly sure.

Because the adaptation is half-hearted, however, this psychologised motivation merges into something more nearly existential when the scene shifts from Sicily to Tunis, and Leonido is temporarily cut off from contact with Marcela. He declares that he does not wish to think, but to "observe my processes as well as I can". [40] And when he does attempt a self-assessment, it is as an object of the experience of others. The following speech occurs after his reunion with his sister in exile, but it is addressed to her only in Leonido's "distracted" imagination:

Where are you? Where's your timorous Dionisio? Where is your *memory* of me? It shall soon fail. My imprint will have died out of all hearts inside a month. Discard. A discard. I have been mostly, a fair mixture of intelligence, mostly, self-criticism and, yes, gullibility. Yes, that's a hesitating assessment. [51]

The final four sentences are in Osborne's typical introspective-heroic vein—and oddly reminiscent of Bill Maitland. But, like much of the interpolated dialogue, they are symptoms of a self-explication which runs counter to the course of the surface action.

A pity, really, that Osborne didn't reject all the trappings of Lope's plot. This would have left him free to write a "serious" version of *Under Plain Cover*—or rather, of that part of its action that the earlier play had hidden behind the closed doors of Tim and Jenny's seven dark years together. As it is, his hero speaks with two mouths. He regurgitates a vestigial something of Lope's theme of payment and redemption—or rather, a theme of payment and restitution, as Osborne's older testament has it. But he also hints at new kinds of causality for his actions, which at times seem attributable to hedonism, and at times to a genuine affection between brother and sister.

This character-relationship is developed fairly fully: but it comprises only part of the play, and not an organic part at that. Probably *A Bond Honoured* is no more possible to realise self-consistently on a stage than is Osborne's opening demand for "actors like athletes who behave like conversationalists". [15] Both surely assume a synthesis more like a curate's egg than an omelette. *A Bond Honoured* has, in the event, proved to be Osborne's last major stylistic experiment, at least for a while. Perhaps it was its failure that caused him also to unlearn the more fruitful lessons of *Inadmissible Evidence* and *A Patriot for Me*, and to revert, in *Time Present*, to the very earliest of his themes and of his dramatic modes.

11

Time Present

TIME PRESENT has a sting in its title. Its actress-heroine Pamela is in fact as maladjusted to the swinging sixties as Jimmy Porter was to the flatulent fifties. But whatever warping of chronological contexts *Look Back in Anger* and *Time Present* may have in common—in their titles as in their themes—some twelve years of a writer's creative development came between their conceptions, during which time Osborne had changed from provincial rebel to metropolitan recluse. The attic-squalor in which his earlier work took place is thus transmuted into anaemic affluence—the change of local-colour reflecting less any chameleon characteristics in Osborne himself than a shifting in that complex of observation and experience on which he could most readily draw. But if instinct was sufficient to spark a dramatic revolution in *Look Back in Anger*, it is not enough to breathe life into the more cerebral world of *Time Present*. The paradox is that Osborne's formal instinct still directs him towards naturalism, although his theatrical temperament now tends to whittle away at a single character until his identity vanishes into the void—the void to which Bill Maitland came at the close of *Inadmissible Evidence*.

Pamela is haunted not by her own past but by her father's: and so, for that matter, was Jimmy Porter. But Pamela is shacked up with no grovelling male squirrel: her flatmate—or, more precisely, her willing hostess—is Constance, a professionally forward-looking female politician of dominating demeanour. The roots of the relationship between these two women are never explored, however. As so often in Osborne's work, an instant-affinity has to be assumed on the slenderest of evidence. Lesbianism is obviously latent: but whereas an audience was plunged into a convincing continuum of marital disharmony in *Look Back in Anger*, here it is asked to believe that the bickering by which Pamela and Constance measure out their stage-lives has merely put some previous understanding "a bit out of kilter". [46] There is no means of plumb-lining this kilter, however: and the continuous wearing-away of the two women at each other's nerves has to be accepted on its own, instantaneous terms.

Thus, Constance replies to Pamela's complaint that she "sounded like a wife" with the wry reminiscence:

We always seemed to like the same things and react similarly. Most women just seem to make me impatient. [34]

Maybe. But there is little evidence of overlapping tastes, personal or sexual, as the characters are conceived dramatically—and Osborne goes out of his way to sum up scenically their essential separateness. His opening description of the play's single set reads:

Constance's flat in Pimlico. For the present she is sharing it with Pamela. There is some evidence that it is lived in by two people with different temperaments and interests. On the whole, the impression is rather severe, more a working area than a place to lounge around. The influence of Constance is in the Scandinavian furniture and abstracts. There is also the evidence of her profession of M.P. There is a wall of books, reports, white papers, volumes of Hansard, Year Books, filing cabinets and hundreds of back numbers of political weeklies, all very neatly arranged for reference. There is a prominent, large Swedish desk covered with still more books, newspapers, reports, galley proofs and a typewriter with paper in it. [13]

Pamela's presence is permitted its corner of untidiness—and is cluttered with the relics of her father's past triumphs on the stage. If anything, this only confirms one's doubts about the inherent improbability of her partnership with Constance. It does not matter that Constance's belief in their compatibility may be mere wish-fulfilment: but it does matter that Pamela—who turns out to be the single character in the play of real dramatic significance—should ever have been inveigled into such a fantasy-friendship

She has a dream of her own: a dream very like Jimmy Porter's, but sustained by the life-style of an actor-father who excelled in awful plays, rather than the glory of a father dying of dedication to a betrayed ideal. She was born in India—an apparently superfluous item of information, yet one which helps to narrow-down her nostalgia to something approaching Jimmy Porter's loving-hatred for a lost imperial past. [23] And Pamela's mother, just like Jimmy's, is fonder of the abstract "texture of life in a Socialist society", [80] than the reality of life with a fallible mortal. There is, however, one essential difference—which the titles of the two plays suggests. Jimmy's father died decades ago. Pamela's dies at the end of the first act: and her retrospection in the second takes on less of the anger of Jimmy Porter than the apathy of Bill Maitland.

Constance's flat is handily situated for the hospital in which Gideon Orme is dying: and it is useful, therefore, as a place in which his family can foregather for recuperation between bouts of sick-visiting. This is why the curtain rises

on two women who are not in residence at all—on Pamela's
mother Edith, and on the teenage daughter of Edith's second
marriage, the pallid Pauline. The ensuing scene between
these two is very nearly disastrous: neither character is fully
realised, for Osborne is concerned much more about factual
than psychological exposition, and for most of the opening
twenty minutes he has mother and daughter filling in background with which both are already acquainted. Thus,
consider the complete subordination of *showing* to *telling* in
the following speech of Edith's, soon after the play begins.
She has just telephoned the hospital:

> Pamela's been with him since eight o'clock. She said he
> was a bit quieter. Whatever that means. He always seems
> to chatter whenever she's there. She lets him go on and
> on then gets more exhausted than ever. By the time I get
> there, he complains all the time about how tired he is
> and can't sleep. Why am I so tired, Edith? I haven't done
> any work for years. Not since I was at the Shaftesbury.
> He even got that wrong last night. That was long before
> the war. He complained all the time just before *I* left.
> Are you sure you want to come? It's not much fun,
> darling. You know, sitting up all night in a hospital
> room. [14]

"You know," indeed: there is little in any but the first two
lines of the speech that Pauline conceivably *cannot* know.
And Edith is not a garrulous gossip prone to such superflui-
ties: she is an efficient divorcee, recognising a duty towards
her ex-husband on his death bed. Her exposition, in short—
unlike Billy Rice's in *The Entertainer*—is extraneous. And a
page later comes this:

PAULINE: Odd fish for Pamela to shack up with.

EDITH: How do you mean?

PAULINE: Oh, I don't know but I suppose she's frightfully intellectual and an M.P. and all that. And—well, I mean, Pamela's an actress.

EDITH: She's not exactly unintelligent, darling. Even if she does get her life in a bit of a mess. And I think Constance has been kind to her and after that last affair bust up and all.

PAULINE: What? Oh, Alec. But that was for years. Like marriage. Worse. [15]

Valuable information, this: but the manner of its giving would suggest—if it weren't for the evidence of *The Entertainer*, *Inadmissible Evidence* and *A Patriot for Me*—that Osborne had learnt little about his craft since the collaboration with Anthony Creighton on the first act of *George Dillon* more than a decade earlier.

Constance duly arrives, and gets the play, though not herself, off the ground. She stands in greater need of dramatic substance than her visitors, since her world and her values are a necessary sounding-board for Pamela's. Of course, Constance is conceived as a comparatively colourless person— her home "more a working area than a place to lounge around"—and her lines are spattered with deadly commonplaces. "I respect and admire you for what you are," she tells Pamela, typically and almost unspeakably. [33] But one gets the feeling that Constance's very dimness is a device to save Osborne from overmuch bother with her—which would be excusable, had her personality not so evidently yet inexplicably attracted Pamela. Neither the obscurely lesbian nature of Constance's feelings towards her house-guest, nor the impulses that move her as a person and as a politician, are explored. She is a useful butt for Pamela's bitterness, as she is for occasional onslaughts against her parliamentary vocation—but these merely parody Constance's point-of-view, because they *reflect* only Pamela's.

The gap between Constance the polemicist and Constance the person is never measured—and is often assumed to be non-existent. Thus, consider the moment when Pamela comes across the draft of a pamphlet on which Constance has been working. It is called, credibly enough, *Striding into the Seventies with Labour*, prompting Pamela to remark:

> Striding into the seventies. I haven't got used to hobbling about in the sixties yet. Give us a chance. [32–3]

And already one's attention begins to shift from the committee-room ring of the pamphlet's title—which is well echoed—to Pamela's mockery of its implicit challenge. Then comes the following exchange:

> CONSTANCE: It's very easy to poke at people who are trying to cope realistically with the future. And glib.
> PAMELA: But what about the meantime? We've got to get through that, haven't we? I don't know about striding off anywhere. I seem to be stuck here for the moment . . . that's not being glib. We have to wait up . . . not be able to get to sleep . . . it's strange how easily men seem to get off to sleep . . . always before you . . . off . . . and you wake up tired . . . but not in the seventies . . . Tomorrow . . . that's early this morning, *this* morning. [33]

Constance talks like one of her own pamphlets: but Pamela responds like herself—and this at a moment when what might have been a crucial and meaningful difference between them comes to the surface of their conversation. In fact, Constance offers us no convincing explanation of her commitment to time future, so that Pamela's difficulties with her own decade are given free theatrical rein.

There are several other symptoms of Osborne's lack of interest in the political side of his play. Edith is even allowed to commit the unpardonable solecism of referring to the "*New Humber and Fisheries Development Act*. Second reading" [15]—a stage at which no measure aspires to be more than a Bill. That Osborne lets this pass, and later permits Pamela to emend the "act's" title when she picks up the same order paper, [32] reveals not only a characteristic unconcern for verisimilitudinous detail, but also Osborne's sheer lack of interest in Constance's occupation. It is not, of course, obligatory for any dramatist to concern himself with parliamentary politics—unless, as in the case of *Time Present*, he has *chosen* to write a play in which they assert a claim to prominence. As it is, the all-too-evident cursoriness with which Constance's career is treated distorts the ostensibly naturalistic perspective of *Time Present*.

Having saddled his play with its naturalistic trappings, however, Osborne faults himself at nearly every fence. His characterisation of almost every person except Pamela—of Constance, Edith, Pauline, and of the motley crew of men who waft in and out of the flat and of the lives of its occupants—is no more than sketchy. It is, though, a sketchiness such as the formal shape of *Inadmissible Evidence* could have contained. For in that earlier play, Maitland's neurosis was rendered in all its subjective totality: but in *Time Present* the surface realism prevents an audience from getting under Pamela's skin—and also from taking the more cardboard characters in a sort of solipsistic stride. This becomes all the more puzzling at the play's climax—for it is Constance, not Pamela, on whom the curtain falls. Like Maitland, she is alone at the end of a telephone wire. Pamela herself has departed—first for a chaste visit to her homosexual agent, thence to the isolation of her own home:

> I shall go back to my little house and one day I shall pick up the telephone when it rings. And if it doesn't ring, never mind. I may have to ring someone else instead. If they're in . . . [62]

This anticipation of what Pamela eventually intends to do is very close indeed both in manner and matter to Maitland's climactic realisation that the telephone and his own life have been simultaneously cut off. But in *Time Present*, the concessions to naturalism modify the play's finality. Pamela goes off with her agent, who is indisputably flesh-and-blood, and the final curtain falls, inexplicably, on Constance instead.

Of the male members of the cast-list there is very little to be said: indeed, *Time Present* is unusual not just among Osborne's works but among most modern drama in being peopled entirely by women for almost half its length, and in therefore permitting its men to play purely functional parts— to be precise, of impregnating or helping to abort Pamela. Among these males, there is Murray, who turns up at the end of the first act as Constance's lover—and who eventually becomes Pamela's, in one of those instant-affairs Osborne likes to develop during his intervals. There is Edward, a sort of universal boy-friend, who crops-up to react with a mixture of tact and embarrassment to the news of Gideon's death. And there is Bernard, the homosexual agent, who makes an appropriately gay appearance to hump baggage and serve as chauffeur on Pamela's departure. None of these characters is given much to say, nor very fully realised in saying it. But one is inclined to accept the lack of sub-stantiation in their cases *because* of this subordination of their roles. They are there not to talk but to act—even to the extent of "getting a girl in the family way", true to George Dillon's time-honoured convention, in the final act.

But Pamela, more worldly-wise than George or Josie, plans to abort her indiscretion. And Osborne, with rather less dramatic wisdom, allows her telephone arrangements to be overheard—not just once, on Murray's over-convenient entrance, [60] but a second time, by Constance, who doesn't even make much use of the information. [73–4] Murray at least has the decency to enquire "Oh, Pamela, what's happened to us?" true to his role as cast-off lover. [61] These over-timely entrances, together with the opening expository scene, turn out to be the only major *structural* defects in the play. It is, of its kind, "blessedly well constructed", though not in the sense that Pamela gives to the phrase:

> That means it's like a travelling clock. You can see all the works. That way you know it must keep the right time. [70]

The "works" of *Time Present* are, on the contrary, relatively well-concealed—it is in its characterisation and, to some extent, in its thematic development, that it is flawed. True, Osborne still insists on drawing attention to pseudonymity, getting Pamela to "forget" the name of

> that woman—what is she, in the Treasury—the one with the teeth? [31]

and, in truly impartial spirit, then allowing Edith to refer to

> that man in the opposition Front Bench. The one who's so hot on the arts. You always see him at Covent Garden. [54]

However, such lapses into over-demonstrative pronouns are mainly interesting for their rarity. *Time Present* has its faults, but they are much less *obtrusive* than the faults of *George Dillon* or even of *Luther*. Osborne has the tools of his trade under much better control: it is the new material to which he applies them that proves less tractable in *Time Present*.

Of course, there are the sideline sports which Osborne finds it hard to resist in any play. Pamela shares her author's hatred for theatre critics to the point of paranoia. "You have to be frigid to be one of them," she remarks, and later adds aggression and timidity to her diagnosis. Indeed, she gets quite heated about the sex-life of reviewers—or rather the lack of it:

> As for them, there's something fundamentally wrong with you if you want to do that. Something missing. I've noticed it. When you meet them. Impotence. That's why when they've been really nasty, they try to ingratiate if you're ever unlucky enough to meet one. [71]

As a practising critic, I'm not sure whether I prefer to be accused of frigidity, or of the lecherous-blackmail widespread in the profession according to Tom Stoppard's *The Real Inspector Hound*. But that isn't really the point: it is simply unfortunate that, however well-integrated such a slander against the critical confraternity may be into Pamela's general waspishness, her attack is too much in her creator's personal vein of polemic for her not to *seem*—justly or unjustly—to be reduced by such remarks to a spittoon for authorial spleen.

This is just a single example of a thematic confusion which pervades the whole play. And having defended Osborne against the unjustifiable equation of his own views with those of such characters as Jimmy Porter and Bill Maitland, I

don't think I'm falling into the biographical fallacy in suggesting that such an identification is harder to avoid in *Time
Present*. Of course, Osborne has always allowed his characters to go off at obsessive tangents, and one often senses a
certain, but not a *central* authorial sympathy with these
obsessions. Fair enough: it brings them more fully to
dramatic life. In *Inadmissible Evidence*, Maitland's jealousy of
youth was part of *him*, and therefore part of the play. In
Time Present, Pamela's opinion of the young is equally
derisive: yet it lacks subtlety and, worst of all, the play's
naturalistic shape demands that her disgust be given some
moving targets—in this case her step-sister Pauline and, in
particular, a rival actress named Abigail.

Pauline's hip-jargon floats in the air, lethargically begging
to be pin-pricked by one of Pamela's barbs. Consider this
quarrel over an unseen hippy hanger-on called Dave, whom
Pauline has dumped in the lobby:

> PAMELA: Just send him back where you found him. Where
> was it? The Sidcup Rave Cave. Yes?
> PAULINE: Get lost, draggy.
> PAMELA: I'll get the law, if you don't move, darling.
> EDITH: Oh, stop sniping at the girl, Pamela.
> PAULINE: We just do fun things, so what's the matter with
> *you*, then? [24]

Draggy, fun things—words and phrases which demand
deflation. And elsewhere Pauline talks about a "rave up"
[14] and the "different scene" to which her step-father be-
longs. [17] This jargon had lost its life even before the play
was first produced at the Royal Court in May 1968, and in
a future revival it is going to sound distinctly coy. But what
makes the matter more serious is Osborne's apparent intention that Pauline's philosophy of life should *complicate* the

dramatic issue, not over-simplify the alternatives it proposes. And this intention does come into focus during the long-postponed appearance of Abigail towards the end of the second act. [74–8]

Now, Abigail is also an actress, but not of the tradition which Pamela has inherited from her father. And the references to her earlier in the play anticipate a drama-school version of Pauline:

> Abigail: just because she's made a movie and someone's talked about the mystery behind her eyes. She's got no mystery behind her eyes, she's just myopic which enables her to be more self-absorbed than ever and look as if she's acting when she's just staring at wrinkles on your forehead. [37]

That colonic caesura separates the object of scorn from the cumulative force of the definition which follows it. But the speaker could as well be George Dillon, Jimmy Porter, Archie Rice or Bill Maitland as Pamela, pausing to vent her vituperation to best effect. After a perfunctory objection from Constance, she continues the attack:

> She moons about on street corners in a French movie, looks listless and beautiful in her own big, beady way while you hear a Mozart Requiem in the background. She plays with herself, gets the giggles while she's doing it and they say she's a cross between Garbo and Buster Keaton. Abigail—who's never seen a joke in her life when it was chalked on a blackboard for her, who was the only person in the entire world who didn't know the truth about her Daddy until she found him tucked up with a Greek cabin steward and the family's pet bulldog! [37–8]

Now this convoy of triple-decker blunderbusses is by no means the last to run down Abigail in her absence. Deliberately or otherwise, Osborne builds up a word-picture of a character painted by her instinctive enemy—as George Dillon daubs the Elliots in their true bourgeois colours, or as Bill Maitland creates a verbal action-painting on the blank canvas that is his daughter. But in Abigail's case it is a portrait drawn from a memory the audience has not shared: and until her belated entrance there is no means of judging whether Pamela's attacks are valid—or whether they are "just vicious", as charged by Constance. [43]

In fact, Abigail proves to have a zest for living which, however malformed by prevailing pop fashions, cannot but clash with Pamela's own increasing sense of dissociation. If only Osborne had given continuous force to this conflict his play's outward realism might have made formal and thematic sense. Formal sense, because Abigail is *not* a character conforming to a subjective impression of herself, like Jane, but a real and vital contrast to Pamela. And thematic sense, because it is with the broader implications of this contrast that *Time Present* is most of all concerned—the contrast, in a nutshell, between Pamela's self-conscious, cultivated "style" and Abigail's "instantaneous" instinct for living.

Abigail is Madeline in the flesh—Jimmy Porter's Madeline, whose "curiosity about things, and about people was staggering", and who was able to relish "simply the delight of being awake, and watching". But it is too easy to say that Pamela is *jealous* of Abigail: rather, she reacts against the girl's embodiment of all that Pamela rejects as contrary to the life-style inherited from her father. This doesn't matter. What is important is the sudden sense of conflict that Abigail's entrance and her brief, explosive scene generate. Afterwards, even Pamela has to give some ground:

Why does Murray want her for his play? At least she's
alive in her way. Even he gets bored with his dollies.
The thing about them is they really are mostly wooden.
Abigail isn't wooden. [78]

Abigail certainly isn't wooden. She's alive—*in her way*: and
that way is crucially different from Pamela's. But it is only
near the end of the play that this difference begins—as far
as the audience is concerned. The rhetorical dice have been
loaded in Pamela's favour, and so radical is the readjust-
ment required to Abigail's last-minute arrival that there just
isn't enough time to get both characters into a common
focus before the curtain falls.

The play adds up more in retrospect than in the immediacy of its performance. At last the recurrence of Pamela's
allusions to "style" makes sense—not just as a symptom of
her nostalgia, but as the cause of a living conflict between
two generations. Jimmy Porter, like Maitland's mirror image
Maples, was unable to remember feeling young. Maitland
himself was at once attracted and repelled by youth. And
now Pamela, approaching forty, finds that her own allegiance to a dying way of life cuts her off from time present.
She hobbles about in the sixties while Abigail dances. And
her equal detestation of Pauline suggests that her contempt
is indiscriminate. She baits her step-sister, and, *in absentia*,
her step-brother Andrew—whose willingness to share the
sick-visiting is put down to his wish to enjoy "a bedside
happening all to himself". [22] Like Abigail, Andrew comes
in for a lot of criticism: but unlike Abigail, he never makes
an appearance. Maybe the ambiguity here is deliberate.
Thus, of Pamela's four youthful victims, Abigail is as much
envied as hated, and is demonstrably worth more than the
word-picture painted of her. Andrew and Dave may or may
not deserve the contumely heaped on them—and Pauline

does earn her own measure of disgust, even before Pamela appears to give voice to it. Unfortunately, her scorn for youth never sticks to anyone *except* this caricature of a teenager—this embodiment of adult prejudices, who is unable to act in her own defence.

Pamela's dislike of Pauline works negatively, therefore, in the same way as George Dillon's contempt for the Elliots. She conforms to a conventional mould too perfectly to be quite true:

> PAULINE: You don't know it yet, Pamela, but you'll wake up to it, all your scene is really out, and it'll be out for good and you with it.
> PAMELA: I think you're right.
> PAULINE: Those draggy plays. Who wants them?
> PAMELA: Who's arguing?
> PAULINE: Oh—you're just camp.
> PAMELA: So I've been told. Just like my father. [25]

Just like her father: such an affinity is Pamela's human shortcoming and her histrionic strength. Even Edith feels closer to her younger children:

> *We're* not friends. She and I, I mean. Well, certainly not like Pauline and Andrew and I are friends. In an odd way, we three seem to be more like the same generation. We understand each other. Perhaps it's just the old problem of remarrying and having more children. [20]

Not at all: the "old problem" is actually that of the alienated middle-generation, amongst whom Osborne has so often sought his "exceptional" central characters. In Jimmy Porter's case, the alienation was compounded of nostalgia and introverted class-consciousness, and it was purged by the controlled contempt of Jimmy himself. Pamela seeks a similar kind of consolation. But her nostalgia is not for proletarian innocence: it is for an indefinable quality called "style", with which her father—a sort of legit version of Billy Rice—swept through his stage career, and to which she opposes the "vulgarity" of time present.

One of Pamela's main objections to youth is that it has become "hideously self-conscious and ugly". [24] In other words, it lacks style, pure or applied. Style can redeem such ugliness, apparently—as it redeemed the succession of hack plays in which Gideon Orme starred, and from whose yellowing reviews Pamela is prone to quote. She compares her father with Edith in these terms just before the final curtain:

> The old man had more in the way he held a tennis racket than every letter she ever wrote to the papers. From unemployment in the Highlands to bed wetting. [80]

Pamela thus prefers posture to political involvement. And, in a riposte to Constance's accusation of her unfairness towards Abigail, she also assumes style to take priority over sense:

> Ah, Constance, like so many people you don't understand the content of tone of voice. You're like an American, you have no ear. All voices are the same to you. It's only what is said that seems significant. [43]

Tone modifies content—or, contrariwise, exaggeration is excused by inflection, for which Murray, like Constance, is accused of having no ear. [48] And consider the implications of the following exchange:

PAMELA: I think excessive effort is vulgar.

CONSTANCE: Thanks again. Is that part of your high Toryism? It's a little shopsoiled. That kind of romancing and posturing I mean.

PAMELA: I think there's a certain grace in detachment. [43]

This is the obverse of Jimmy Porter's anger—a perpetuation not of a long-lost commitment but of the "cool" detachment which Pamela goes on to claim for her father:

He was cool. Pauline and Dave think they're cool. But you can't be cool if your sense of self and, well, ridicule is as numb as *theirs*. [43]

This could be Bill Maitland's indictment of Jane—who is similarly accused of taking no pleasure even in the infliction of pain. But Pamela's fundamental hatred is of vulgarity—of which she condemns such diverse occupations as dieting and sun-bathing within a couple of lines. [56]

She even talks of her father's death in terms of its "timing", [53] and in this sense the whole play amounts to an exercise in her applied feeling for theatricality. This, or so Pamela considers, makes all the world a stage:

I think Murray's one of those intellectuals who thinks all actors live in a narrow, insubstantial world, cut off from the rest of you. Well, kid yourself not. You're all of you in Show-Business now. Everybody. Of course, Orme was never in Show-Business. Books, politics, journalism, you're all banging the drum, all performers now. [48]

This is another familiar theme, of course: and, as in *The Entertainer*, there can be no apter setting for a play about the cultivation of personae—of the show-business variety, or of

Gideon's higher breed—than a theatrical one. "Everyone," Pamela has claimed a little earlier, "thinks actors have got no brains and live in some world walled up from the realities everyone else is immersed in". [35] And again the irony is double-edged—both by and against Pamela. She has brains enough: but she *does* live within her own and her father's walled-up world. Dramatically, those walls could have been better constructed from the inside, as they were in *Inadmissible Evidence*. Or they could have been more fully contextualised, as they were in *The Entertainer*. But *Time Present* falls between these two stylistic stools: it sets Pamela within an ostensibly realistic environment, but forces no objective contrasts between character and action—at least, until Abigail's appearance. Then the latent conflict at last comes to life.

Thus, contrast the limp verbiage which is the best Constance can muster with this representative effusion of Abigail's:

ABIGAIL: Then we saw a bit of some Swedish movie. It had some thrilling things with a girl having a baby.
PAMELA: Really?
ABIGAIL: I thought it was rather beautiful. But Eddie got bored and fell asleep and I woke him up, and we bought these super records. And, oh, yes this, well, we thought it would be fun if I changed. You know, there's a picture of me in every paper today. So we dropped in at Wig Creations for the moustache, then got a taxi to Carnaby Street. Walked all the way to Charing Cross Road. Not a head turned. Isn't it marvellous? [76–7]

Now the quality of the life to which this exuberant prose—as careful in its slight hesitancies as in its confident connectives —refers is arguably paltry, and it is certainly "fashionable" in the worst, colour-supplement sense. Yet the quality of the *person* here plunging into such a life is considerable. It is in pointing this kind of paradox that *Time Present* at last struggles towards an incisive conflict—and towards an ambiguity in the portrayal of Pamela herself which could profitably have been amplified at an earlier stage of the action.

Among the incidental digs that Pamela's profession enables Osborne to get in, there is this description of the absent Andrew's artistic proclivities:

He's very keen on a lot of American plays, sort of about leaving nude girls in plastic bags at railway stations. Non verbal, you understand, no old words, just the maximum in participation. [46–7]

A palpable hit—at happenings if not at Andrew. Now Osborne himself admits to sharing Pamela's distaste for the happenings-school—understandably so, for his own drama-turgy depends on the manipulation of words as its mainstay, and generally accords them priority over actions, even of a conventionally "theatrical" kind. But an audience's "partici-pation" in *Time Present* is very much too limited: for of the characters who make any major contribution to the play, insight is gained only into Pamela as a person. And this is achieved *because* Pamela's stage-life—and only hers—is inte-grated in a verbal and physical sense. Consider, for example, the relationship between language and character in this advice to Murray about his future with Constance:

You will find each other. Or not. I don't want to talk about it. I won't be involved in your life, or hers. I'm sorry for both of you. *Not* much. A bit. You'll manage, so shall we all. Just remember: what I should do now or at any time is nothing to do with either of you. I owe you no confidence. [63]

The succession of short sentences—each amplifying the last, but adding up to a whole that is as disjointed as the thought-processes discernible in the degree of overlapping—suggests Pamela's introspective mood. Words are coming reluctantly, and relate to what she already regards as an irrelevance. But her more consecutive outbursts show her "performing" in full rhetorical flood no less clearly. Just a couple of pages later the tone has changed to one of truculent polemic:

Do go, Murray. I want to get undressed and I feel shy with you about the place and Constance will be back and it's quite clear you're longing to tell her. Well, I can't stop you. But I don't want her solicitude and being practical and sustaining all of us. I'm quite practical enough for myself. And I don't want to sustain all of us. Even if you two do, and I know you will. You're all bent on incest or some cosy hysteria. She's bound to blub. You're not above it, and we'll all end up on the floor embracing and comforting and rationalising and rumpled and snorting and jammed together and performing autopsies and quite disgusting all of it. You both are. Don't indulge her. Just because she demands it. [65]

The gradations of meaning here have the casualness of a free-flow that is in fact under careful control—of a speech, in short, that is increasingly acted rather than spoken, as style gradually asserts itself over instinct.

Here, finally, is Pamela describing a different attempt at controlling language, in a moment of confession to Constance:

I tried writing love letters to someone. For quite a long time. Then I found my handwriting was getting like his. I don't know what I can go on saying. I love you. I need you. I want you. I ache for you. I need you beside me and in my bed. Don't let's part like this again. It's more than I can bear. It's never been like this in my life before. I never thought it could be. . . . I tried writing erotica to him. But I couldn't bring myself to send it ever. I'd write it down, pages of it. I'd like to. I want you to . . . I dreamt that. . . . Then make up a dream. But it was too explicit. And then it seemed impersonal. Puritanism, I expect you'd say. [44]

This is the point at which "style" finds itself stifling spontaneity. It *is* puritanism of a kind—an inversion of Jimmy Porter's social puritanism. And it is symptomatic of Pamela's refusal of reciprocity—her refusal to give herself up to a lover's identity, or to adjust to any values other than her father's. She is straitjacketed within her life-style, just as *Time Present* is straitjacketed within its dramatic form. For both the character and the play this constriction has damaging consequences—though Pamela herself, rising on a rhetorical flood above the sea of supernumeraries, has the tragic potential of a Bill Maitland. It is a niggling naturalism which hems her in, and which distorts her own identity in the interests of an abortive breeding of lesser characters.

12

The Hotel in Amsterdam

THE HOTEL IN AMSTERDAM is a statement about an existing emotional situation rather than a developing action. Here, Osborne has worked more strictly than in any of his earlier plays within the boundaries of a "given" complex of human relationships—and has thus avoided the element of incongruity in such arbitrarily motivated alliances as those between George Dillon and Josie, between Jimmy Porter and Helena . . . or between Pamela and Murray in *Time Present*. There is no real conflict in *Amsterdam*, and no necessity for one. A couple do, admittedly, declare their love for each other: but their confession turns out to change nothing, merely putting into words an affinity that both have sensed for a long time. And at the play's climax, a man does commit suicide—but he dies off-stage, just as he has been pervasive in his physical absence throughout the action. It is this man, K.L., a film director whose initials always suffice to identify him, from whom three couples draw together in a bid for sanctuary. Their escape-route ends at a hotel in Amsterdam —a refuge in which they plan to enjoy at least one weekend free from the man whose influence or authority more or less dominates each of their lives.

In the drawing-room of their hotel-suite, the six talk, drink and make plans. In the first act they have just arrived: in the second they are about to depart. This "action" defines their mutual dependence, but does not *develop* it: and only the climactic death of K.L. threatens to disrupt the pattern of friendship woven into their weekend. There is none of the bickering and compulsive backbiting of the "friends" in Osborne's other plays—from the rough-and-tumbling Jimmy and Cliff in *Look Back in Anger* to the abrasive Pamela and Constance in *Time Present*. These half-dozen characters in a hotel-room deflect all hostilities towards the absent K.L. Amongst themselves, amity and amiability reign. For most of the time they slump in their easy chairs, sip drinks, gossip, and think about seeing the sights. They are an in-group, revelling (probably with an unwonted self-consciousness induced by the escapist weekend) in their ability to rub along together:

> LAURIE: Here's to all of us. All friends and all together.
> MARGARET: Well, naturally.
> LAURIE: No, it's not natural. It's bloody unnatural. How often do you get six people as different as we all are still all together all friends and who all love each other. After all the things that have happened to us. Like success to some extent, making money—some of us. It's not bad.
> GUS: Bloody good.
> LAURIE: Everyone's married couples nowadays. Thank heaven we're not that. [98]

Laurie is making wedlock mean what he wants it to mean, of course. All three couples are actually married—but they are not exclusive or withdrawn in their partnerships. Osborne has never written about a bunch of characters so relatively well-adjusted—adjusted, that is, not to any socially-imposed norm, but to each other. *The Hotel in Amsterdam* is not only a sedentary play for its characters: it is a restful play for its audience—at least until its final ten minutes. "I say, this is *good*, isn't it," asks Gus: [111] and although his companions are less prone to verbalise their pleasure, none of them disputes it.

The Entertainer excepted, this is also Osborne's most successful attempt to render with a degree of emotional realism a balanced group of characters rather than a hero around whom action and actors gravitate. True, Laurie has more to say for himself than the rest: but his verbosity suits his profession as a writer, just as the relative taciturnity of Dan befits his own role as a painter who has opted to exile himself from the working class. Gus, the third man in the party, is a rare example of a fully-drawn Osborne character who is almost excessively normal, yet entirely sympathetic. A film-editor by profession, he is prone to a certain public-school heartiness, but he also has a redeeming knack of self-deflation. Extraverted, organising, childishly benign, he is the antithesis of the self-analysing, indolent yet waspishly witty Laurie: and to the one's physical hypochondria is opposed the other's sense of spiritual malaise. Their friendship has the authenticity of its incongruity.

The women are less well-defined, less readily distinguished. Amy, besides being personal secretary to the ubiquitous K.L., is married to Dan. Annie is Gus's wife, and no less fond of him than she is in love with Laurie—whose own wife, Margaret, is in the early months of pregnancy. The play's success depends very much on how well these interrelationships work: for there is little more than their unravelling to its plot. And what little more there is might best have been dispensed with, if it could not have been integrated more satisfactorily into the action. Of the two interjections into what otherwise constitutes a conversation-piece, the least excusable takes the distraught form of Gillian—Margaret's younger sister, who descends towards the middle of the second act, in the throes of an unspecified and, as it transpires, an irrelevant emotional crisis. Apparently, her presence is intended to put the party to some sort of test, for Gillian herself does no more than simulate jollity, burst into tears, and retire to be solaced by her sister. [129–32] It is as if the group is meant to be defined in part by its exclusion of such outsiders—as it is also defined by its common dependence on K.L. Thus, Gillian is said to be "not one of us" precisely because "she's not really anything to do" with the dominating director. [114]

This flip-sided definition of friendship gives Osborne the focus for contempt his central characters always seem to need. Yet K.L.'s eventual suicide, the second arbitrary disruption of the weekend, at once undermines the foundations of the friendship, and proves it to have been—evidently to the group's surprise—as crucial to the film-director's existence as he has been negatively necessary to its own perpetuation. The suicide, one feels, should either have shattered the calm at an earlier stage—in which case the fragmentation it seems to anticipate could have formed the substance of the second act—or not at all. Structurally, what might have constituted the middle-act "development" of a three-act play is in fact its conclusion: and in consequence *The Hotel in Amsterdam* resolves itself into a loose-end.

With the rather special exception of *Inadmissible Evidence*, *The Hotel in Amsterdam* is the only one of Osborne's plays so nearly to adhere to the neo-aristotelian unities of time and place. Such pseudo-classical rules can, of course, often be more legitimately broken than observed: but they are useful as disciplines, if nothing else, and Osborne is a dramatist who finds the imposition of such a formalised shape upon his plays at once difficult and profitable. Thus, as in *The Entertainer*, he has integrated his exposition successfully into his action by treating it as a kind of shared compulsion to talk. Going over the old grounds of their friendship comes naturally to this in-group—on a special occasion that seems to *demand* the taking of emotional stock. In particular, the six friends can relish their present escape better by talking about it—and they are usually seduced into such self-consciousness by Gus. It is he who interrupts Laurie's elaboration of a bright idea about airlines for homosexuals—a motif that is to recur several times during the play—as follows:

> GUS: It's not bad is it? I say, we're getting our wind back aren't we? Just starting to feel safe I suppose.
> DAN: We're really here.
> LAURIE: Really here.
> ANNIE: I don't know who's more astonished that we've all scarpered. Us or whether *he* will be.
> AMY: K.L. will be *pretty* astonished when he finds out.
> MARGARET: Let's face it: so are we.
> ANNIE: We do sound a bit amazed at our own naughtiness.
> LAURIE: No, we're not.
> MARGARET: Yes, we are. Come on. You are.
> LAURIE: No, we are relieved, unburdened, we've managed to slough off that monster for a few days. We have escaped. [92–3]

As usual, the idea of escape connects irresistibly with the image of the person from whom the group is in flight. Margaret's comment is pertinent:

> How amused he'd be. Here we are congratulating ourselves on escaping from him and we've hardly stopped talking about him since we left Liverpool Street. [94]

But the talking has, quite incidentally, filled out the background shared by these six refugees: and, substantively, it has suggested the function of K.L. himself, as the gravitational force keeping his underlings in their common orbit—despising his petty demands, but ultimately dependent on them.

An enormous quantity of alcohol is consumed in *The Hotel in Amsterdam* as, indeed, it was in *Time Present*. In that earlier play the staple drink was champagne—appropriately stylish, but a sedative to Pamela's jangling sensibilities all the same. In *The Entertainer* it had been gin, which at once induced a temporary solace and stimulated an incessant, sometimes maudlin flow of family-consciousness. Now, in *The Hotel in Amsterdam*, it is whisky, and it encourages conviviality. The play is, in essence, a long, discursive session of small-talk: and it is by the quality of the talk that it must be judged. Interruptions need to illuminate what is *said*, because so little in the play depends on what is *done*.

In this sense, Gillian's arrival is potentially fruitful, for it exposes the in-group to the pressures of adaptation. But adaptation to what? Gillian's troubles are made no clearer than her character. Admittedly, Margaret declares herself

> worried about that girl. She's my sister and I love her, and I think she came very close to doing something to herself this weekend. [142]

But then comes the second interruption—the telephone-message conveying the news of K.L.'s death—and no more is said on the subject of sisterly suicide. Gillian is a kind of *dea ex machina*, in short, but her presence doesn't even arbitrarily clarify the action: it arbitrarily complicates it. Gillian has broken "the fragile spell", as a stage-direction puts it, [131] but the jagged edges of the shattered mood are never allowed to cut deep.

K.L.'s suicide is evidently more integral, and it gives a vicious twist to a tale of interdependence that has previously been ironic. But there is even an off-putting attempt to link Gillian with the dead director. It was, apparently, from her that K.L. wheedled out the whereabouts of his lost legion: and this asserts itself as a blatant bit of over-structuring in a work that is otherwise almost free from the convenient coincidences of patchwork playwriting. [141] The *timing* of the suicide—even closer to the final curtain than Abigail's arrival in *Time Present*—makes it, moreover, a means of manipulating the characters off the stage rather than a purposeful development. Osborne seems to feel an obliga-tion to *make things happen* in his plays—even in *The Hotel in Amsterdam*, which is most truthful at its least consequential, and at its tritest when it is trying to be "theatrical".

Character, then, is revealed in conversation rather than in action. There is a temptation, therefore, to get drawn into fruitless comparisons between the opinions of Laurie and his creator, simply because Laurie is also a writer—and, as a compulsive talker, the obvious candidate for that "central character" who had given equilibrium to Osborne's earlier plays. Sure enough, there is some of the compulsory critic baiting by Laurie:

> I'm certainly not spoiled. I work my drawers off and get written off twice a year as not fulfilling my early promise by some philistine squirt drumming up copy, someone who's got as much idea of the creative process as Dan's mother and mine rolled into one lazy minded lump of misery who ever battened off the honest efforts of others. [99]

But this is tinged with irony—and even self-deprecation:

> I'm an impoverished writer with a wife, children, useless servants, a family of ageless begging letter writers, a

trencherman nanny and three dogs as big as you. I
haven't yet found my voice, I write too much not enough,
I have no real popular appeal, I take an easy route to
solutions— [131]

Laurie, in fact, is unique among Osborne's characters in his
ability to keep his tongue both in check and, on occasions,
in cheek. The familiar hobby-horses are thus ridden at an
unusually gentle pace—and because this is atypical, it
saddles them with Laurie's rather than his creator's imprint.
More important, because they extend not only to such
authorial sports but to everything Laurie says, are the conversational counterweights of the other characters. These six
people know each other too completely for dissimulation, or
for choosing words with undue care and attention: their
reciprocity is not sustained by good taste or by tact, but by
the instinctive mutual adjustments of intimacy.

Osborne describes his three couples in an opening stage
direction as:

fairly attractively dressed and near or around forty but
none middle-aged. In fact, they are pretty flash and
vigorous looking. [87]

Now this is interesting. Here is a middle generation not
looking back in nostalgia—well, not overmuch—but loung-
ing back in luxury. It is the unfortunate and unrealised
younger sister, Gillian, who now opts for unhappiness: and
her appearance is both belated and brief. Laurie, at least, is
said to have been "loving friends for ten years" with K.L.
[109]—suggesting a degree of environmental stability, to
which the evident happiness of the three marriages adds an
emotional assurance.

It's not quite as simple as this, of course, for Annie and

Laurie are as much in love with each other as with their respective spouses, and the revelation of their relationship is arguably the only true "development" in the play's static progress from Friday to Sunday. The couple's temperamental sympathy has never been in doubt: but neither has the love with which each continues to regard husband and wife. Earlier, Laurie has held forth on the subject of romantic love:

> LAURIE: Yes. I read somewhere that one of those communications people, the men who tell you what it is we're all feeling now because of *the* media, said that marriage and romanticism was out. At least with the young people.
> ANNIE: I suppose it was on the way out when we came in.
> LAURIE: I wonder where we ought to go to live. All those sleepy-eyed young mice squeaking love, love. Scudding into one another, crawling over each other, eyes too weak for bright light, tongues lapping softly . . . all for love, a boy's tail here, a girl's tail there, litters of them. [118–19]

Again, there is the familiar rasp of ridicule for youth—but none of Maitland's or Pamela's jealousy is mingled with it, for Laurie, as it turns out, enjoys both married and romantic love. Sexually, his faltering declaration of his affection for Annie, and the platonic future both seem to anticipate, may beg important questions: but rhetorically the scene is entirely convincing.

Laurie has been married before, and here he describes a sense of creeping dissociation under which earlier Osborne heroes would have been crushed:

> LAURIE: You live with someone for five, six years. And you begin to feel you don't know them. Perhaps you didn't make the right kind of effort. You have to make

choices, adjustments, you have requirements to answer.
Then you see someone you love through other eyes. First,
one pair of eyes. Then another and more. I was afraid to
marry but afraid not to. You see, I'm not really promis-
cuous. I'm a moulting old bourgeois. I'm not very good
at legerdemain affairs. . . . Do you like Margaret?
ANNIE: Yes . . . Have you been unfaithful to her?
LAURIE: Yes. [139]

Under gentle questioning—which one cannot imagine a
Jimmy Porter or a Pamela either needing or tolerating—
Laurie elaborates his confession. Then Annie asks him why
he has chosen to tell her.

LAURIE: Why? Because . . . to me . . . you have always
been the most dashing . . . romantic . . . friendly . . .
playful . . . loving . . . impetuous . . . larky . . . fearful . . .
detached . . . constant . . . woman I have ever met . . .
and I love you . . . I don't know how else one says it . . . one
shouldn't . . . and I've always thought you felt . . . perhaps . . . the same about me.
ANNIE: I do. [139–40]

The whole scene repays detailed examination: but at these
moments of epiphany it is at its most revealing. Laurie's
painful sense of the need to accommodate his instinctive
puritanism, the adjectival preamble which *is* his description
of Annie, and their shared sense that their avowals need no
elaboration: in all this, embarrassment is blended with self-
confidence, complexity with simplicity, in a manner that
exactly predicates the couple's physical relationship on a
stage. At once intimately certain of each other, yet groping
towards the verbal expression of their certainty, Annie and
Laurie could no more fall into each other's arms at its

achievement, in a dramatically demonstrative manner, than they could set about talking-the-whole-thing-over like adults of the playing-it-cool school. There is nothing to talk over, no further step to be taken. The *status quo* has not even been disturbed: its nature has merely been acknowledged.

Gus is all this while in the bath. He is, thankfully, no such straight-man as Cliff, and even cultivates his obsession for organising and his healthy hypochondria as much to amuse his friends as to indulge himself. He has brought more baggage than anyone, and is uncomfortable without his street-map. He has a tendency towards over-explicitness, and towards draining an emotion by analysing it—but even in this weakness lies a kind of pathos:

> Really escaped, didn't we? I haven't laughed so much for months. Have you, darling? You said last night. [123]

The speech-rhythms here are inimitably Gus's—quite different from the elliptical Laurie's or the laconic Dan's. These two are happy to take things more or less as they come: but Gus has an organising humour. He plans everyone's routines for them, but isn't really cut out for impromptu weekends:

> I need a bit of looking after, I'm afraid. I hate staying in other people's houses. Unprepared and all that. No shaving stuff. Or someone else's. And I don't like really sleeping on my own. Somehow, well the quality of sleep is different. Do you know what I mean? [105]

Dan doesn't: he can sleep anywhere. But Osborne's own sympathies have broadened since the caricaturing of Brother Bill and Graham Dodd, so that Gus's amiable stolidity at once varies the course of the conversation-flow, and forms

an insuperable—because innocent—obstacle to any further-
ance of Annie and Laurie's feelings for one another. Annie's
constancy is the final item in Laurie's catalogue of her
qualities, and it is not in doubt.

That the remaining three characters are less caught up in
the emotional vortex only vitalises their dramatic function—
as leavening, at the lowest level, and as less complex personalities who nevertheless assert a simple humanity at the
highest. Dan and Amy have relatively little to do or say:
yet their inactivity is itself integral. The pregnant Margaret
is less attached to her husband than Annie is—and less
tolerant of his fits of verbosity. But she is also more conventionally loyal, and she thus exerts a strong stabilising
influence. Dan, similarly, works at "a controlled pace",
[108] and he draws on a kind of spontaneous energy which
Laurie—acutely self-aware—can only envy:

> Dan doesn't need energy. He runs perfectly efficiently on
> paraffin oil. You fill him up once a year and he's alight
> for another twelve months. With me, I need the super
> quality high-thing stuff poured into my tank twice a day.
> [103]

These "six people as different as we all are" make up for
each other's deficiencies, draw on each other's strengths.
And, it is hardly necessary to add, their differences make
their roles in a conversation-piece such as *The Hotel in
Amsterdam* much more supportable: six characters each as
strong as Laurie, and shade to shade would come too tire-
somely. What matters is that the remaining characters are
not the functional automata who surround Pamela in *Time
Present*, but precisely the sort of people likely to draw
together in a defensive alliance against their ubiquitous
employer.

Gus is "always taken by surprise by situations and people's reactions". Laurie "rehearses them all". [125] And, as Dan later comments, with unwitting aptness:

The trouble with being spontaneous, or even trying to be, and I think one can, the trouble is it does put you at the mercy of others. [128-9]

Laurie does not, however, take advantage of the less well-rehearsed Gus. He out-talks the others, but he never upstages them—either as an individual, or as a character in a play. This is because Osborne has caught exactly the sense of give-and-take within his tightly-knit group—a remarkable advance for a playwright whose previous successes had almost entirely depended on his ability to discover a formal shape for accommodating a succession of solitaries.

Thus Laurie, even in the fullest flood of his verbiage, talks *with* rather than *at* his companions. It's not until near the end of the first act that he is allowed anything approaching a monologue: and this is a hymn of hate on the obsessive theme of K.L. It even anticipates, with a dramatic irony unusual in Osborne's work, the director's suicide at the close of the second act.

Go on, go on playing the big market of all those meretricious ambition hankers, plodding hirelings, grafters and intriguers. I simply hope tonight that you are alone—I know you won't be. But I hope, at least, you will feel alone, alone as I feel it, as we all in our time feel it, without burdening our friends. I hope the G.P.O. telephone system is collapsed, that your chauffeur is dead and the housekeeper drunk and that there isn't one con-man, camp follower, eunuch, pimp, mercenary, or procurer of all things possible or one globe trotting bum boy

at your side to pour you a drink on this dark January
evening. . . . [117]

The state of loneliness "as we all in our time feel it, without
burdening our friends" proves unbearable—not to Laurie
and his companions but to K.L. himself, a "dinosaur" seen
only through the distorting mirror held up by his reluctant
hirelings. The paring-down of a life to the nothingness at
the core of *Inadmissible Evidence* and *Time Present* is here taking
place off-stage.

"I suppose we all play different roles to the dinosaur. But
they're still roles," comments Gus. [93] But it is for K.L.'s
deception that their several masks have been moulded—so
that amongst themselves, and therefore undisguised, the
characters in *Hotel in Amsterdam* come closer to knowing each
other than do the dramatis personae of any of the earlier
plays. This is not to say that they necessarily know *themselves*
any better than Jimmy Porter or Archie Rice: but at least
their search for self-knowledge is shared, and the deceptions
that remain are mutual. One such deception is suggested by
their fear of airing too openly the suspicion that K.L. may
be a necessary catalyst to their friendship. Gus ponders on
the possibility:

GUS: The trouble is he creates excitement.
LAURIE: Not half enough.
GUS: Perhaps we're all second rate and need second rate
excitement, sort of heats one's inadequacies. [117]

And this launches Laurie into his first monologue of the
play. It begins as a desperate rationalisation of the relationship with K.L., in which all the taking is on the director's
side, and all the giving is on theirs—and the piling-up of
collocative phrases and of simple synonyms is intended to

G

reassure rather than convert his hearers by its cumulative conviction.

This kind of phraseology is, in fact, a consistent, carefully observed speech-habit of Laurie's—which he indulges most fully in his adjectival eulogy of Annie. He likes, too, to invent verbal-motifs which become running gags around which the in-group can improvise—notably, the idea of El Fag, the airline for homosexuals, and the creation of the Golden Sanitary Towel Award for Gillian's supposed sufferings. The whole group falls into the kind of jargon that may sound merely whimsical to outsiders—they always go for a zizz instead of taking a nap, and even commit the ultimate bourgeois euphemism of referring to a woman's periods as "the curse". Laurie's later monologues are perhaps over-indulgent, but each—the parody of a letter from a scroung-ing relative, [126] the ode to Australian nurses, [128] and the slightly jaded joke about the silent nun [134–5]—gives its own kind of counterpoint to the situation, and is generated by it instead of seeming an interpolated set-piece.

The ambling direction taken by the to-and-froing dialogue is also naturalistically convincing as well as dramatically purposeful. Thus, in a random couple of pages, [90–1] it drifts from drink to travel to class distinction, from families to mothers to homosexuality—and from there into the foundations of El Fag Airlines. [92] Laurie's remarks tend, indeed, to be slightly longer, and much more assertive, but this merely accords with his character, and does not diminish the human stature of those who let themselves be harangued. As Laurie puts it:

> I love Gus very much. I think he really believes most people are better than him . . . I only suspect it. [120]

This is probably as good a contrast as any between the

pair—the two male characters who make the strongest dramatic impression. It doesn't matter whether Laurie really believes this himself. That he calculates his effects is conceded: but *what* he says, true or false, is an expression of a need as deep as K.L.'s for the security of togetherness. He wishes, or so he claims, that he could live alone:

> It can be all right for weeks on end even. But then. You have to crawl out of the well. Just a circle of light and your own voice and your own effort. . . . [119]

Laurie has given up trying: he needs other people, and he admits his need.

It is in this negatively-stated theme of loneliness that *The Hotel in Amsterdam* forms a natural group with *Inadmissible Evidence* and *Time Present*, just as *Look Back in Anger* and *The Entertainer* were linked by a common theme of looking back. True, nostalgia remains a temptation, at least for the men-folk, but it is usually resisted—as Annie reflects:

> You sometimes try and fumble your way back to child-hood while we watch and get impatient and wait for you to stop. [130]

Osborne's dramatic preoccupation is no longer with such retreats into times past, but with the problem of reconciling oneself to time present. Neither Bill Maitland nor Pamela achieved such a reconciliation, and tragedy hedges about the climax of *The Hotel in Amsterdam*. But the tragedy seems somehow separable from the preceding action: it is, maybe, more a warning to the remaining friends than a prophecy of impending disintegration. Certainly, three-quarters of the play points to the possibilities of mutual adjustment, and accepts a measure of self-deception as a small price to pay for friendship. Perhaps the play marks not so much a turning-point as a resting-place in Osborne's dramatic career, as this one weekend does in the lives of its characters.

13

A Note on Osborne's Journalism

JOHN OSBORNE is a good playwright, and potentially a great one: if I didn't believe that, I would certainly not have bothered to write this assessment of his work. The end-product he will no doubt cordially despise: for he is jealous of his privacy, and understandably so. It took him a long time to lay the ghost of the angry young man, insubstantial shadow though it always was: and this ghost I have no intention of resurrecting. So in the analyses of Osborne's plays in the preceding chapters, there is scarcely a reference to their author's private life or opinions: but in this penultimate section it has been necessary to invade the one area of his personality which Osborne has *chosen* to make public property—namely, that which distinguishes him not as a creative artist, but as an occasional critic of his society, and of his fellow workers in the theatre.

As a dramatist, John Osborne is humane, insightful and compassionate: but as a commentator, he can be as vitriolic, half-truthful and intolerant as any member of that monstrous regiment of critics he condemns. And the causes of this apparent schizophrenia are worth examining. Osborne himself admitted its symptoms long ago, in the credo he contributed to *Declaration* in 1957:

> Whenever I sit down to write, it is always with dread in my heart. But never more than when I am about to write straightforward prose, because I know then that my failure will be greater and more obvious. There will be no

exhilarating skirmishes, no small victories on the way to defeat.[31]

Osborne's "straightforward prose" is usually exhilarating—but it can also be painfully muddle-headed. Maybe this is because he turns out prose reluctantly and to order—but writes plays at his own pace, and to his own inclination. At least, the one exception, the commissioned adaptation of *A Bond Honoured*, certainly seems to prove such a rule. For Osborne is an instinctive writer, whose *theatrical* instinct can usually be trusted. And yet as a playwright, he is necessarily at one remove from his text: he is writing across the identity-gap that separates him from his heroes—the frequent facile equations with whom he rightly rejects. But as a polemicist he is attempting to transmute feelings into ideas, instincts into abstractions, with a directness uncontrolled by a formal discipline. And he is not much better at this than the hack reviewers he hates.

One of the earliest of Osborne's journalistic adventures was a review of six plays by Tennessee Williams, which he contributed to *The Observer* early in 1957.[32] "There are," it began, "too many critics. I have no intention of setting up in the appraisal business." This was to become a familiar kind of disclaimer and, inevitably, a false one: for it is no more possible to distinguish a "critical" appraisal from a playwright's personal opinion in Osborne's case than it was, say, in Bernard Shaw's. Nevertheless, Osborne's "appraisal" of Tennessee Williams is revealing: it confesses a disciple-ship, and a shared desire to assault

the army of the tender-minded and tough-hearted, the emotion snobs who believe that protest is vulgar, and to be articulate is to be sorry for oneself; the milk-in-first phlegm boys who will mine meanings from seams that

fell apart years ago, but will summon up all their dis-
engaged hostility, all their slicked-up tired old journalistic attitudes, and get into a pedantic, literal-minded
flap over inessentials when they are forced to look at a
slum or a bombed site (these two really seem to hurt for
some reason) all the evening—or, worse, at the kind of
homes millions of people have to live in.

This attitude of mind Osborne neatly encapsulates as "the
adjustment school of criticism". And he spends the next
three paragraphs of his review attacking it.

In many ways this short notice is as pertinent a piece of
criticism as Osborne has ever written: it defends the dramatist's right to people his plays with neurotics rather than
"normals", and it defines "sex and failure" as Tennessee
Williams's dramatic themes. They are also, of course,
Osborne's: and it is revealing to find him suggesting such
an affinity at this stage of his career—when *Look Back in
Anger* was still widely regarded as a representative play of
its generation, not as a study of a very exceptional character
indeed. Osborne's *Observer* review is full of fine, memorable
phrases. "Even Aunt Edna has an itch under the tea tray,"
it proclaims: and maybe it is because its proclamation is so
positive—a declaration of dramatic faith, in which the abuse
of the "adjustment school" is both relevant and deserved—
that it has remained Osborne's most convincing excursion
into the critical arena.

A few months later Osborne answered, along with eight
other writers, a questionnaire sent out by the *London Magazine*. The assembled replies were dubbed *The Writer in His
Age*,[33] and they were—true to their time—mainly concerned
with the issue of "commitment". Osborne believed that
"most writers appear to be indifferent to the problems of
human freedom" because they were "surrounded by inertia

at home". The relative affluence of "most ordinary working people" did not create "the kind of atmosphere" that produced "the heart-searchings and the gestures of the 'thirties". As a dramatist, however, Osborne declared an "unequivocal" sympathy with a proletariat that had in fact been "dumped on an ash-can as dirty and as dangerous as the old one". This ash-can was full of "cultural, emotional and spiritual rubbish", and with its occupants Osborne felt a need to communicate, "without compromise and patronage".

This was probably the period in which Osborne came closest to advocating "commitment"—not a commitment to Jimmy Porter's "causes", however, but to people. Later in the same year, he contributed his long article to *Declaration*, between whose covers he found himself rubbing shoulders with such spiritual opposites as Lindsay Anderson, then on the far left, and Colin Wilson, on his own outsider's right. Anyone who actually read this symposium in its entirety could never again have credited the existence of such a corporate "angry young man" as it seemed to embody. The rest—who did not read it, but noted the names of its contributors—were merely reassured that they did, indeed, represent a movement and a mood.

They Call it Cricket was the title given to Osborne's contribution, which remains to date the fullest statement of his beliefs available in print.[34] Whether the beliefs themselves remain is another matter. Having "dreaded writing this piece", Osborne admitted that "the people I should like to contact—if I knew how—aren't likely to be reading this book anyway". And at the very end of his article he returned to his ash-can theme. Rejecting any intention of solving social problems, he ennumerated "the questions of socialism" which a creative artist such as himself should be asking about ordinary working people—questions such as these:

What is their relationship with one another, and with
their children, with their neighbours and the people
across the street, or on the floor above? What are the
things that are important to them, that make them care,
give them hope and anxiety? What kind of language do
they use to one another? What is the meaning of the
work they do? Where does the pain lie? What are their
expectations? What moves them, brings them together,
makes them speak out? Where is the weakness, the
loneliness?[35]

Now I am not the first to note that Osborne has never really
tried to investigate these kinds of questions in his plays.[36]
But I don't think he should be blamed for what amounts to
a limitation of artistic range rather than a shrugging-off of
responsibility. His single attempt to write about ordinary
people, in *Epitaph for George Dillon*, was, after all, a dramatic
failure, and any further excursions into the milieu of the
"normals" might have been just as dead-ended. What is
important, in the light of Osborne's later opinions, is the
need he then felt to touch the lives of ordinary people—a need
which, albeit negatively, expressed the extent of his "commitment".

The rest of the article in *Declaration* is much more characteristic: its anger is directed against Britain's first test of a
hydrogen bomb, against royalty-worship, against the ponti-
fications of the posh-weeklies about "angry young men", and
against the established church. There is an autobiographical
digression into Osborne's early life—and a casual hit at the
critics who were to become the blackest of all the *bêtes noires*
in his later journalism:

Most good actors have the humility to admit when they
are floundering in the dark. There are few critics who

would not be better for the same dose of honesty in their
morning tea. But then you can't be expected to know
much about art if most of your time has been spent in
assessing art that is scarcely on speaking terms with the
facts of life as known and felt by the great mass of people
in Britain today.[37]

Again, it is interesting to note Osborne's assumption—which
he explicitly denies at the beginning of his article, confessing
that the people he wants to reach are likely to know him only
as a "rather odd looking" angry young man—that he himself *is* on "speaking terms with the facts of life as known and
felt by the great mass of people in Britain today". The
contradiction is characteristic of a desire for empathy with
the working-classes that Osborne never did infuse into
his plays—and to which he has since abandoned his
claim.

Almost all of Osborne's subsequent polemics have been
about the theatre. But a couple of exceptions are worth
mentioning—the *Epistle to the Philistines*, and the notorious
but widely unread *Letter to my Fellow Countrymen*, both written
for *Tribune* in the early sixties, and reprinted—conveniently,
though somewhat anachronistically—in John Russell Taylor's
Casebook on *Look Back in Anger*.[38] The two are complementary
attacks on social and political hypocrisy—the *Epistle* a kind
of anti-catechism, ridiculing religion, Rolleiflex cameras and
royalty, and the *Letter* an apocalyptic vision, burning with
hatred for "those men of my country who have defiled it",
and who will be responsible for its imminent destruction.
These pieces both approximate to poetry rather than
polemic: they share a sinuousness of feeling and a sharp
economy of language that transcends their ostensibly
"occasional" purpose. They are topical only in conception—and in so far as they no longer typify Osborne's

feelings towards his country, which he has come to regard with an affection that is less patriotic than pragmatic.

Over the years, Osborne's writings about the theatre have become at once less theoretical and more cursory. The introduction he contributed in 1957 to the now defunct *International Theatre Annual* amounts to an affirmation of faith in the form, and it is expressed with an optimism lacking in his later criticism:

> I love the theatre more than ever because I know that it is what I always dreamed it might be: a weapon. I am sure that it can be one of the decisive weapons of our time. We, who work in the theatre, have power, and we should never underestimate—as we do—the extent of that power. We may not have the immediate range of those who are in films or in television. Our power is concentrated. The people who work in these mass media look to us. Usually, we have been found wanting.[39]

Osborne proceeds to defend what the adjustment-school of critics dismiss as "self-pity" and "sentimentality"—in other words, "being articulate about your feelings". But there is some evidence of Osborne's own brand of sentimentality—which might roughly be defined as being articulate about what he'd *like* other people to be feeling:

> I have learnt more about theatre from old women in public bars and upstairs concert-rooms all over England than I shall ever learn from reading the left and right reviews on a Friday. The theatre must be based on care, care for how people feel and live. We haven't got it in England. Perhaps, one day we shall, and then there will be a new strength, new hope and new *care* everywhere.[40]

"Care for how people feel and live" had not noticeably increased in the English theatre two years later, according to an article Osborne wrote for *Tribune* early in 1959, as part of a series entitled—in view of the subsequent general election, somewhat ironically—*Advance on the Left*.[41] Here, Osborne described how the theatre establishment had set about assimilating the recent revolution at its gates:

> Three years ago, the English Stage Company was sneered at for being *avant garde* and eccentric. Now it is sneered at for being "fashionable"—a breathtaking form of belittlement, coming as it does from people who have consistently dedicated themselves to being nothing else but fashionable. This is the whore's scorn for virtue, like the familiar Tory trick of looking amused and civilised and dismissing your opponent as "old-fashioned".

And he concluded:

> Between them, the theatrical managers and the majority of critics have resisted every fresh current of life introduced into the theatre. There is nothing to suggest that they will not go on doing so. It is true that they are uneasy; but the fact remains that they are still where they were before, doing very nicely in their twin Easy Streets, east and west of the Temple Bar. . . . You still want to be a revolutionary? You've plenty of time. The party has scarcely started.

But Osborne himself has become less and less of a revolutionary. Just two years later, in an issue of *The Twentieth Century* given up to the theatre,[42] he repeated his warning against "safe, apparently high-minded middle-brow plays which make all the *gestures*", in their attempt "to promote a synthetic version of the really new theatre, with all its teeth drawn''. His vision of that new theatre, however, had changed:

What do I want for the theatre of the 1960s? First, decent conditions for people to work in, and decent theatres built by architects who know something about it. But what I would like most of all—although of course it's not something you can legislate for—is to see artists in the theatre being allowed to *play* at their work. Everything has to be so serious and specific all the time, and people are continually under the pressure to improve on their last work, to do it perfectly every time, to create a success. The element of *play* seems to have gone out of life, but artists have the right to relax, to be frivolous, to indulge themselves in their work.

By this time, Osborne had apparently resigned himself to writing for an intellectual élite:

It's not my job *as a dramatist* to worry about reaching a mass audience if there is one, to make the theatre less of a minority art. So much of that, in any case, depends on other factors like new buildings with good restaurants, service and other amenities. If you're going to do what other people think or say you ought to do, it's a waste of time. Ultimately, after all, the only satisfaction you get out of doing all this is the satisfaction you give yourself.

No wonder that he concluded by acknowledging:

I'm not really equipped to talk about what I'm doing and what I've done—especially about the things that are furthest away in time. I daren't pick up a copy of *Look Back* nowadays. It embarrasses me.

Thus, a mere six years had wrought a considerable change in Osborne's theatrical beliefs. He had begun as a writer trying to tap the sensibilities of ordinary people. Now he was appealing for a self-satisfying frivolity. And his confidence in *Declaration* about his intentions in *Look Back in Anger* and *The Entertainer* had been reduced to a confession of his incapacity as a critic of his own plays.

Increasingly, he became instead a critic of the critics. Actually invited to stand in for the regular reviewer of the *Sunday Telegraph* during 1966, he devoted his column[43] to a sustained attack on the critical profession, which is revealing in its assertion of a total dichotomy between the practitioner and the critic:

> After nearly twenty years of agitating and trying to create affray from within my own profession, I still cannot contemplate going over to Them. By Them I mean the acknowledged enemy, the critics, most particularly the daily newspaper critics, acknowledged cheerfully and openly by all but a few sleepy pear managements and some truckling actors.
>
> Theatre critics should be regularly exposed, like corrupt constabularies or faulty sewage systems. Indeed, as the structure of institutional theatre grows, I would employ gentle, subsidised chuckers-out so that most daily critics might be barred from openings altogether, along with actors' agents and boxes of chocolates.

"Sometimes," Osborne added, in direct address to his enemies, "it is hard indeed to believe you have ever been instructed in any pain, absurdity or distress."

Another thing: it may be comforting to know that you are unloved and unwanted but you would be wrong to con-gratulate yourselves. You could well become obsolete. You still need to amuse and inform some of the time. Some of us no longer have that obligation, even though we may occasionally observe it.

It is sad and strange to recognise the old, objective anger thus turning-in protectively upon itself. Osborne bears a legitimate grudge against those who did, indeed, mis-represent and misunderstand him—but what a monument of misrepresentation and misunderstanding he himself has raised to the rankling memory! How obsessive the theme has become, and how its language limps along, in bathetic contrast to the wide-ranging denunciations and the blistering prose of the earlier articles.

Twelve months later Osborne returned to the attack. 'The people who write about the English theatre,'' he began, in a composite book-review contributed to *The Times* in October 1967,[44] "are a sad bunch." Unfortunately, his own article was as sad a piece of "writing about the theatre" as any tired overnight-notice, sub-edited out of existence. Ironically, in view of his article's onslaught upon the "seekers after the bare approximate", Osborne cites the bare approximations of two English theatre critics to back up his own views: and it is just this habit of practising precisely what he preaches against that has come to flaw most of Osborne's unfortunate forays into the field of criticism.

On this occasion, a book of interviews with playwrights and directors, co-edited by myself,[45] was among the works singled out for slaughter—an odd choice, since it was at least an attempt to clarify the points-of-view of theatre practitioners, and thus to avoid the "presumptions . . . and bullying guessing games" of criticism-in-a-vacuum. "One can't help feeling," Osborne, however, couldn't help feeling, "that the editors are longing for the writers and directors to shut up and let *them* get on with it." Now if my colleague and myself had really wanted to "get on with it" we could quite easily have done so: but, more to the present point, Osborne's comment is significant in its assumption that the critic is a kind of usurper—a parasite upon the theatrical profession who diminishes any production upon which he preys.

Now far be it from me to deny that certain kinds of journalistic criticism *are* diminishing. So, for that matter, are certain kinds of playwriting, though John Osborne's is blessedly not among them. But his less fortunate experiences with newspaper reviewers have seemingly blinded him to the fact that considered criticism of the theatre—as, indeed, of music, ballet, or any of the arts which are auto-destructive by their nature—is as vital to its future as good acting, directing or, for that matter, good playwriting. There should be no such cleavage between creative artist and critic as Osborne is here helping to widen. The dramatist interprets human experience: the critic interprets artistic experience. Both exercise above all the faculty of selection—of distinguishing what matters from what doesn't. And both can be right or wrong—or, more probably, open to correction and argument.

Osborne had in fact turned down, with great politeness, our request to include an interview with him in the collection he was later to review so impolitely. So, in "getting on with it myself", I am acutely conscious that I am indulging in what Osborne regards as an illegitimate and predatory occupation. But theatre has, of course, always been the most collaborative of art forms, and I believe that the critic has his own part to play in the collaboration. The responsible critic both records and reacts. It is his duty to preserve for posterity as accurately as he can the nature and quality of performances and productions, for these are necessarily ephemeral: but he must also *respond* to them—as anybody responds to works of art, but in the hope that his own feelings and, perhaps, his specialist training may throw off tangential insights, and encourage a meaningful discussion of the nature of particular theatrical experiences. It is then up to the playwright, the director, or any lay member of an audience, to condemn the *quality* of the discussion—for the critic is in as much need of informed criticism as the creative artist. But that the practice of criticism is in itself both necessary and legitimate is a contention I would defend as hotly as Osborne defends—for example—his right to personal privacy.

This apologia would not, perhaps, have been necessary if Osborne had been better treated by the press and the pundits in his early years as a reluctant celebrity. One still senses a kind of compensatory violence, half retributive and half pre-emptive, underlying his rare excursions into journalism. But it is for the best that these outbursts are no longer channelled into his plays—as they were into *Slickey*, *The Blood of the Bambergs* and *Under Plain Cover*. That Osborne has lost most of his old interest in communicating with the masses, and with making the theatre contribute to socialist weaponry, is, indeed, dispiriting. But this, at least, has made very little difference to his development as a dramatist—however single-tracked it has made his increasingly per-functory statements in print. His plays continue to stimulate, and to exhibit that compassion which he might try turning, when necessary with the other cheek, upon his critics.

CONCLUSION

Conclusion

Osborne's major plays have never ceased to be the "lessons in feeling" he first proclaimed them: and those few which have had an ulterior purpose have deservedly been the least successful. *The World of Paul Slickey* and *The Blood of the Bambergs* were excursions into musical and political extravaganza: and they failed not only in their chosen comic styles, but in contorting themselves into formal shapes which were too orthodox for intended onslaughts upon orthodoxy. *A Subject of Scandal and Concern*, on the other hand, in contradiction of its own narrator's claims, demanded a cerebral judgement from its audience—which it ostensibly discouraged, and for which it failed to assemble adequate evidence. And *Under Plain Cover* lost its theatrical way as soon as its own lesson in a certain kind of sexual feeling got sidetracked into a personal lesson Osborne was trying to teach the press.

These several kinds of failure suggest, albeit negatively, that Osborne is a dramatist who works best within certain limitations: but that his failures have been infrequent, and belong mainly to the earlier years of his dramatic career. This hopefully confirms that he is learning either to transcend or to work within those limitations—which probably have to do with temperament rather than technique. For as a craftsman Osborne has grown out of several immaturities which flawed—though in these cases not fatally—his other early plays. His single more recent artistic failure, *A Bond Honoured*, had a significant genesis: it was a commissioned work and an adaptation, whereas Osborne is an instinctive writer who finds it hard to work within even such negotiable boundaries as Lope's text imposed. He thrashed about thematically with his inherited script, tempering its philosophy and its moral implications—but not so fully as to make the play his own, or to conceal the outlines of the renaissance masterpiece beneath the existential overlay.

Osborne is not, then, a dramatist who is ready or, perhaps, able to compromise. He made a mess of *A Bond Honoured* because he tried to accommodate an outside source—and he failed to be funny in *Slickey* and *The Blood of the Bambergs* because contact between the author and his raw material was too close. He could not, in short, achieve the one kind of compromise he finds not only acceptable but necessary: the compromise that occurs when an author sets up a strong central character or group of characters, and becomes at once emotionally committed and yet formally detached from them, thus maintaining the crucial distinction between critical and total empathy.

What I described earlier as the identity-gap—the gap separating Osborne from his central characters, which is bridged but not silted-up in the act of creation—is apparent in all of the dramatist's most important work. It separated Osborne from Jimmy Porter, just as it was later to cut him off from Laurie in *Amsterdam*—and, in between, from George Dillon, Archie Rice, Martin Luther, Bill Maitland and Alfred Redl, as, indeed, from Pamela in *Time Present*. This roll-call of names itself suggests how broad has been Osborne's spectrum of characterisation in successive plays: but it is a reminder, too, of the mental and rhetorical force the characters have in common—and which they would have *too much* in common, but for the one vital remove from which their creator conceives them.

There are, of course, certain directions in which Osborne

has been unable or unwilling to develop. Thus, trials and errors have deterred him from making further experiments in comedy—musical or otherwise—since *The Blood of the Bambergs*. For his undiluted sense of humour tends to be too furious to be funny: whereas, filtered through the objectified play-acting of an Archie Rice, or the sardonic sensibility of a Laurie, it adds its necessary dimension to Osborne's "serious" dramas. He is no more lacking in humour than Ibsen—but neither is he any better at being amusing-to-order. His comedy demands, in short, organic assimilation. Unadulterated, it can sour the sweetest of tempers.

Osborne has never entirely broken the habit of over-structuring his plays. That he can work the necessary business of exposition well enough into a naturalistic sequence of events is amply demonstrated by *The Entertainer*, by *The Hotel in Amsterdam*, and by the first act of *Look Back in Anger*. That he is equally liable to let it sore-thumb its way into his action *Epitaph for George Dillon*, *Time Present*, and the *middle* act of *Look Back in Anger* bear all too eloquent witness. These expository successes and failures make no chronological sense: so it can only be assumed that Osborne reverts to being a well-made dramatist in the worst sense when he is unable—or can't be bothered—to set up a situation which *requires* a mood of retrospection, or to fashion a form, such as that of *A Subject of Scandal and Concern*, which interpolates its narrative element straightforwardly into its text.

Overplotting can also mar Osborne's work. He has three times got that girl of Barney Evans's into the family way in his final act. And a compulsion to inject action into a naturally static situation has haunted him from *Epitaph for George Dillon*—in which George's tuberculosis and his first wife tied for top marks in irrelevance—to *The Hotel in Amsterdam*, in which the arrival of Gillian proceeds to beg all the questions it might have helpfully raised. But the drag ball in *A Patriot for Me*, redeemed though it is by its supreme theatricality, is the grossest blunder of them all, for it is not only disproportionately interruptive to the plot, but a violation of the character of Alfred Redl—who is introduced almost apologetically into the transvestite proceedings.

But Redl, in any case, jumps from stage to stage of his sexual development like a pederastic grasshopper. And in almost all of his plays Osborne has shown a similar disinclination to *develop* a sexual relationship in front of his audience. Thus, at the openings of the first and third acts of *Look Back in Anger* he is willing enough to explore fully-matured stages in the development of Jimmy's marital and extra-marital relationships: but he prefers to let each stage *consolidate* itself during an audience's ice-creams and scotch-and-sodas. It, too, then becomes a "given" situation, ready for its dramatic definition. In consequence, the *least* "developed" plays are usually the best. *Epitaph for George Dillon* and *Look Back in Anger* both have emotional hiatuses, while George and Josie and Jimmy and Helena get into their sexual strides. And *Luther* and *A Patriot for Me* jerk as erratically between psychological states as they do between their historical settings. But *The Entertainer* and *The Hotel in Amsterdam* do not have to "develop" in any such senses, either in time or in the temperaments of their characters: whilst *Inadmissible Evidence* and *Time Present* work their changes retrospectively, exploring backwards in time as their central characters move forward towards self-destruction. It should be noted that Osborne has never mastered the episodic style—or at least, adapted it to his own purposes, of conceiving a fuller social context for a single character. In consequence, he delineates the environments of *Luther* and of *A Patriot for Me* far more fully, and with more justifiable self-containment, than the men those environments should be helping to shape—and his *Bond Honoured* works most arbitrarily of all, revealing neither periods, places nor persons in any depth, but developing each along its own parallel line, which has been tortuously separated out from the inexorable, single-track movement of Lope's original.

No less arbitrary, though somehow more forgivable, are those authorial sports which recur with predictable regularity at every opportunity: notably the stabs of derision at the monarchy and the press in the earlier plays, and an increasing love-hatred towards the young in the later. Osborne's antipathy towards dramatic critics has, however, been recently the hardest ridden hobby-horse of all. But it must be added in all fairness that none of Osborne's marginal quarrels has taken over a whole play since *The Blood of the Bambergs*: and if his journalistic broadsides against the critical confraternity have purged him of an incipient *World of Milton Hobson*, then they are minor wounds eminently worth the bearing.

Maybe Osborne's hatred of his reviewers has something to do with his reluctance to remedy the defects in his own craftsmanship—which are mostly slight, measured against the assurance of his total dramatic structures. His earlier press notices in particular—before his commercial success began to be accorded its invariable respect—tended to sneer at the hypostasised anger of his heroes, and to treat each successive play like a symptom of some lurking threat to the British way of life. But rebutting such non-criticism need not have left Osborne so anxious to defend rather than learn from his real mistakes—the fracas over *A Bond Honoured* is the classic case of such over-reaction to adverse criticism— and to pay a mite more attention to the details of his craft. He can now be certain that unjustified abuse will meet its deserts at other hands than his—as Kenneth Tynan, for example, slapped down Mary McCarthy's uncomprehending attack upon *A Patriot for Me* in *The Observer*.[46]

Of course, there are dangers in advising a dramatist like Osborne to take lessons in dovetailing details, or in expediting his exposition—at least, there would be dangers, if there were any likelihood of his heeding such advice! A balance is certainly hard to strike. Tied up in knots of constructional knick-knackery, much of the spontaneous vigour of his plays—which are generally put to paper quickly, after a long period of gestation—might be lost. Perhaps most of all, therefore, he needs a strong director, and preferably one with a certain skill in play-doctoring—not of the anaesthetised kind that takes place at transatlantic seminars in creative-writing, but of the kind to which Arnold Wesker, for example, submitted at the hands of John Dexter during the rehearsals of his own early plays, and which he now gratefully acknowledges. In Osborne's equally suitable cases for treatment, *The Blood of the Bambergs* and *A Bond Honoured*, however, Dexter was either less inclined to advise surgery, or discouraged from it by his prospective patient. And self-doctored or not, it's significant that *The World of Paul Slickey*, the only one of his plays directed by Osborne himself, has also been his most unmitigated disaster. At least he appears to have learnt enough from that experience never to try repeating it.

Of the other directors who have worked with Osborne, William Gaskill has a reverence for the text which has worked wonders for Brecht and Farquhar, but which ill-befitted *Epitaph for George Dillon*—whereas Tony Richardson takes such liberties as decked-out *Luther* in ritualistic glory, and which thus buries the faults of a text beneath the business of his own directorial sub-text. It has only been in his most recent director, Anthony Page—who has worked on every one of the plays at the Royal Court from *Inadmissible Evidence* onwards—that Osborne seems at last to have found a man whose mind works not so much at a similar as at a complementary pace to his own. But not even Page could do much for the opening minutes of *Time Present*—which could so easily have been excised—though even a session with Pamela's scrapbook might have made for a more endurable exposition. Page's remarkable sense of Osborne's own timing seems to have given him proprietary rights over productions of Osborne's new plays, however, and one hopes that the partnership continues to prosper. Even the Royal Court Theatre itself—to which has been entrusted all but the premières of *Slickey* and, perforce, *A Bond Honoured*—probably exerts its own kind of stabilising influence upon Osborne: and at least it demands such discipline as a sense of writing to the dimensions and the considerable limitations of that stage can impose.

I have been straying into incidental criticisms of particular productions and thus beyond my self-imposed terms of reference. But this has been in order to suggest what is probably Osborne's only major dramatic defect according to *his own* terms of reference—for within this defect are compounded so many of his minor weaknesses. And this is the kind of instantaneous, take-it-or-leave-it attitude towards his craftsmanship which tempts him to ignore informed or at least well-intentioned advice—and which incidentally diminishes his triumphs by forcing him into over-strenuous defences of his artistic failures.

But whatever the advantages or disadvantages of Osborne's instinctive approach to the manner of his play-writing, an increasingly cerebral orientation in its *matter* has recently been evident. And so has a sense of *social* complexity, such as too seldom counterpointed the personal complexities of the earlier plays. Osborne still writes mainly about "exceptional" people—those whose character traits are writ large, as he once put it, and who are thus, in conventional terms, "neurotic". His single attempt to set such a neurotic person within a "normal" environment, in *Epitaph for George Dillon*, was least convincing at its cosiest, and least acceptable as an acting-vehicle for those cast in its unexceptional roles. Thus, the unspeakably ordinary Pauline in *Time Present* is in a tradition established by the vacuous Norah in *George Dillon*, and continued by Graham Dodd in *The Entertainer*, and by Jones in *Inadmissible Evidence*.

Until *The Hotel in Amsterdam*, even those few "normals" who were conceived as sympathetic rather than self-satisfied —Jean Rice in *The Entertainer*, for example—lacked much dramatic interest. They were not exceptional, but neither were they "interesting"—that is, normal according to standards more engaging than those of the fifties and sixties, as were the long line of leftovers from previous generations from Colonel Redfern to the unseen Gideon Orme. It has thus been the *middle* generation, neither old enough to cling to the certainties of an imperial past nor young enough to retain much hope for their futures, from whose ranks the "exceptional" heroes have generally been recruited. And it has been the upper and the lower classes who have filled in a sufficiently "interesting" background—so that the bourgeoisie have come in for the severest treatment, both at Osborne's hands and from the mouths of his central characters. Except in *George Dillon*, however, they have been least well represented in the cast-lists. Even Osborne's early anti-monarchism, it is pertinent to recall, was directed *in his plays* more against royalty-worshipping middle-class mums than against royalty itself—which was embodied by Princess Melanie in *The Blood of the Bambergs* with as much sympathy as was the journalistic profession by Stanley in *Under Plain Cover* and by the ambiguous Oakham in *Slickey*. It is, indeed, true to say that once Osborne's figures of furious fun have been so dramatised as to become "interesting", they have generally been humanised in the process—and accorded a sympathy such as the uninspiring Elliots could never hope to win.

Thus, only in *The Hotel in Amsterdam*—and with un-expected abruptness after the archetypicality of *Time Present*—was Osborne able at last to render a balanced, mutually-adjusted group of characters. Simultaneously, he was also able to strip away most of the overlay of plot with which he had previously felt impelled to fill out—and some-times to overburden—his plays. I think that *The Hotel in Amsterdam*, in these senses, marks the end of a phase in Osborne's creative development. His early preoccupation with the atrophying effects of rationalised nostalgia—with which Jimmy Porter and Archie Rice were both stricken—had persisted even in *Time Present*. But by this time Osborne's interest had already shifted to alienation of another sort—the existential alienation of the loss of one's sense of objective identity. This was Bill Maitland's estrangement, and the theme of *Inadmissible Evidence*—a theme expressed in a more appropriate *form* than in any of Osborne's previous plays. This same theme was latent, though buried beneath a debris of renaissance leftovers, in *A Bond Honoured*. And then, in *A Patriot for Me*, it was as if Osborne were trying to make out with a telescope what he had put beneath a microscope in *Inadmissible Evidence*: for instead of compressing a world into Bill Maitland's mind, he set Alfred Redl against a broader social tapestry than he had ever before tried to weave—reassembling its military, social and sexual patterns into all kinds of permutations, but permitting Redl himself to pick up threads in none. In that play, however, it was the society rather than the stranger lost in its midst which came to life: but in *Time Present* Osborne again chose to depict a solitary figure in an almost suspended environment, so that Pamela found herself alone against a hazily hostile background of family and friends, and of actors and affluent agents.

Such was the mainstream of Osborne's development until

The Hotel in Amsterdam. In *Slickey*, *Luther* and the *Plays for England* he had been temporarily diverted into other courses —but only to return to surveying the struggle for an honourable reconciliation with self and with society. At last, in *The Hotel in Amsterdam*, that reconciliation seems to have been achieved. The curvature of its action follows neither the well-made semi-circle of *Look Back in Anger*—from exposition to development to resolution—nor the vicious-spiral of a modern tragedy, such as catches up Bill Maitland in *Inadmissible Evidence*, returning the play's action not to its *status quo* but to the beginning of another action in another dimension: the drawing-out of an endgame into a perpetual stalemate. But in *The Hotel in Amsterdam* that tragic action is taking place in the wings, to a life that touches those of the characters very closely, but whose traumatic climax offers them a choice—the choice between asserting a new freedom, or of accepting disintegration, deprived of the common object of hatred which has previously been binding them together.

Thus, *The Hotel in Amsterdam* ends neither on a note of hope, such as is briefly sensed in *Look Back in Anger*, nor in that resignation which is the best *The Entertainer* can offer— nor in the self-destruction with which *Inadmissible Evidence*, *A Patriot for Me* and *Time Present* alike conclude. Although the circle in *The Hotel in Amsterdam* may not be vicious, however, it is, undeniably, closed—both physically, within the four walls of its hotel-suite, and temperamentally, in the exclusiveness shared by its in-group of occupants. But this in-group is not, in Osborne's usual sense, exceptional: it is not cut off from society, nor yet is it slavishly absorbed into it. And perhaps most important, it can exist, talk and act on a common level of assumptions, each member adjusting to the individualities of his fellows.

This adjustment depends, too, on a development in

Osborne's use of dialogue—from its more-or-less conventional to-and-froing in *George Dillon* to the rhetorical filli-bustering of *Look Back in Anger*, and from the more genuine but limited reciprocity of *The Entertainer* to the solipsistic, subjective realism of Bill Maitland's stream-of-consciousness in *Inadmissible Evidence*. Again, *The Hotel in Amsterdam* marks a kind of culmination: for here speech-patterns are neither conventionalised out of recognition, deployed like defensive strategies, nor transmuted into the processes of thought. Language becomes, at last, a mode of communication between characters who mutually accommodate its use to each other's foibles and feelings, and who pick up and volley each other's verbal motifs and idiosyncrasies. This isn't to imply that *The Hotel in Amsterdam* is necessarily a better play, or that it uses language better, than its predecessors: rather, it is a *different* play, and uses language differently—as a medium for understanding, not as a weapon of class or sexual war.

Osborne himself has, thematically, now come full circle as a dramatist. The dubiously talented George Dillon settled down to the mediocre comforts offered by the Elliots and by Josie's animal warmth. The members of the in-group in *Amsterdam* are resigned to their own kind of intellectual affluence, and bask self-sufficiently in each other's glow. They are perhaps kinder and certainly more articulate than the Elliots: and their play closes not on the full stop of an epitaph for themselves, but on the question-mark inscribed on someone else's.

That question-mark hangs, too, over Osborne's future development as a dramatist. That his best works of the past will survive seems to me beyond doubt, especially after the evidence offered by the revival of *Look Back in Anger*, which opened just as this book was nearing completion and which has confirmed my own feelings about the universality of the play's implications—firmly pinned-down though the production was by the fashions of the mid-fifties. Personally, I would nominate *The Entertainer, Inadmissible Evidence* and *The Hotel in Amsterdam* as additional candidates for permanent survival, and would offer *Luther* as a respectable set-text until a new fashion in historical drama catches up with examiners. Of the rest, *Epitaph for George Dillon* and *Time Present* will probably be good for rep revivals for no more than a decade or two. But four plays out of Osborne's first twelve will surely secure themselves permanent places in the international repertoire: and such a proportion is one in which any dramatist can take pride.

It is, of course, now Osborne's *next* play that must be awaited—and, god willing, the many more that may be expected from his pen. Which makes the "concluding" label attached to this chapter a contradiction in terms. It concludes a book, but it cannot sum up a working and developing dramatist's career. This career, truly, seems to have reached a point which future critics may well choose—in their occasionally helpful and occasionally irritating way—to regard as the close of a "period" in Osborne's evolution as a playwright. And that he remains a dramatist who has never consciously plotted a course for himself but who writes as the mood and the moment dictate, makes the anticipation of his next step all the more exciting.

But the immediate present, at least, seems likely to be a time of adjustment for Osborne—and, for that reason, perhaps an opportune moment to offer this interim assessment of his work. I can only add that I have tried to learn Osborne's lessons in feeling—and that I have also accepted his permission to "think afterwards". Maybe my own thinking will help to provoke more written responses—whether supplementary or downright contradictory—to the wealth of feeling, whose surface riches I have just begun to explore.

APPENDICES

Notes and References

Works of which full details are given in the Bibliography are here cited by their short titles only. References to *Casebook* indicate this alternative source for items included in *Look Back in Anger: a Casebook*, ed. John Russell Taylor, 1968.

1 See "They Call it Cricket", 69.
2 *Look Back in Anger: a Casebook*, ed. John Russell Taylor, 1968.
3 See, for example, *Theater of Protest and Paradox*, 233, where George E. Wellwarth claims that "it is doubtful that anything significant can be expected from John Osborne after *Plays for England*. He has become a victim of his own critical success."
4 See *John Osborne: a Brief Chronology*, below, for information about the titles and productions of Osborne's unpublished plays.
5 See Robert Brustein, "Theatre Chronicle", *Hudson Review*, XII, 1959, 94–101. Since then, it should be added, Brustein has come to regard Osborne as a "secondary dramatist". See his *Theatre of Revolt*, 1965, 22.
6 See Kenneth Tynan, *Tynan on Theatre*, 1964, 65.
7 See "They Call it Cricket", 69.
8 Ibid., 65.
9 Ibid., 81–3.
10 See Osborne's "Foreword" to Evans Acting Edition of *Look Back in Anger*, 4.

11 See John Beavan, "Unlucky Jim", *Twentieth Century*, CLX, July 1956, 72–4.

12 See "Swete Alisoun", *Times Literary Supplement*, 25th January 1957, 49.

13 See Osborne's introduction to the extract from *The Entertainer* reprinted in *Writers' Theatre*, 51.

14 Ibid.

15 See "They Call it Cricket", 69.

16 See "Sex and Failure". Reprinted in *Protest*, 270.

17 See "They Call it Cricket", passim.

18 See Charles Marowitz, "The Revolt of Paul Slickey", *Encore*, XI, September–October 1959, 34–6. Reprinted in *The Encore Reader*, ed. Charles Marowitz, Tom Milne and Owen Hale, 1965, 103–5.

19 A stage version of *A Subject of Scandal and Concern* was, in fact, produced in New York in 1965.

20 Born in 1817, the historical George Holyoake became a Chartist at the age of fifteen. By 1840 he was an active member of the Owenite movement, for which he undertook several lecture tours. It was during one such tour in 1842 that he visited Cheltenham, and made the allegedly blasphemous remarks for which he received six months imprisonment. His autobiography, *Sixty Years of an Agitator's Life*, was published in 1892, and he died in 1906.

21 The historical Martin Luther was born in 1483, in Eisleben in Eastern Germany, where he died in 1546. He graduated from the University of Erfurt in 1505, and later in the same year entered the Augustinian cloister there. He celebrated his first Mass in 1507, and was transferred to Wittenberg in 1511, at the instigation of John Staupitz, Vicar General of his Order. A period of increasing theological doubt, during which he formulated the doctrine of justification by faith, culminated in

1517, when he nailed his ninety-six theses to the door of Wittenberg Castle Church. Excommunicated after the Diet of Worms in 1521, he at first encouraged and subsequently helped to crush the Peasants Revolt. He was married in 1525, to an ex-nun.

22 See *Brecht on Theatre*, trans. John Willett, 1964, 70–1.

23 Ibid., 23.

24 See Erik H. Erikson, *Young Man Luther*, 1959.

25 The play opened about two years after the marriage of Princess Margaret to Mr Antony Armstrong-Jones.

26 A note to the programme of the play's first production explains the origin of its title. "It was the Emperor Francis II who first used the term 'A Patriot For Me'. One day, when a distinguished servant of the Empire was recommended to him for special notice, his sponsor remarked that he was a staunch and loyal patriot. The old Emperor looked up sharply: 'Ah! But is he a patriot for me?' The Habsburgs . . . were not interested in German patriotism, in Czech patriotism, in Hungarian patriotism: they were interested only in Imperial patriotism. The army was a body of Imperial patriots."

27 "*A Patriot For Me* is based on fact," states the programme note cited above. "The story of Alfred Redl is true, if not fully known in Austria even today." It may thus be, for example, that the psychoanalyst Shoepfer is not only intended to parody Freudian theories of homosexuality, but to caricature Freud himself, who did his military service as a medical officer in the Imperial Army.

28 See Lope de Vega, *The Outrageous Saint*, trans. Willis Barnstone, in *Tulane Drama Review*, VII, Fall 1962, 58–104.

29 Ibid., 92.

30 See, for example, Angel Valbuena Prat, "A Freudian Character in Lope de Vega", *Tulane Drama Review*, VII, Fall 1962, 44–55.

31 See "They Call it Cricket", 63.

32 See "Sex and Failure". Reprinted in *Protest*, 269–71.

33 Osborne's reply is reprinted in *Casebook*, 59–62.

34 See "They Call it Cricket", in *Declaration*, 63–84.

35 See "They Call it Cricket", 84.

36 Ronald Hayman, in *Contemporary Playwrights: John Osborne*, 79, makes a similar point about this passage.

37 See "They Call it Cricket", 78–9.

38 See *Casebook*, 62–3 and 67–9.

39 See Osborne's "Introduction" to *International Theatre Annual*, II, 1957, 9.

40 Ibid., 10.

41 See "Come On In: the Revolution is Only Just Beginning", in *Tribune*, 27th March 1959.

42 See "That Awful Museum". Reprinted in *Casebook*, 63–7.

43 See "On Critics and Criticism". Reprinted in *Casebook*, 69–71.

44 See "On the Thesis Business and the Seekers After the Bare Approximate", in *The Times*, 14th October 1967.

45 See Charles Marowitz and Simon Trussler, eds, *Theatre at Work*, 1967.

46 See *The Observer*, 18th July 1965.

John Osborne

1929   12th December. Born in a suburb of London, of "impoverished middle-class" parents. His father was Thomas Godfrey Osborne, a commercial artist and copy-writer, and his mother was Nellie Beatrice, born Grove, a barmaid.

1941   Death of his father. Spent much of the war with his mother in London, but was eventually sent to Belmont College, Devon—a "rather cheap boarding school in the west of England", where he was "unhappy for most of the time".

1946   Left school, and had his first play produced: he now describes it as "terrible". Worked as a journalist for a few months on trade magazines—*Gas World* and *The Miller*—as a "a sort of dogsbody and sub-editor".

1948   "Drifted" on to the stage, as tutor to juvenile actors in a touring group. He himself acted for the first time at the Empire Theatre, Sheffield, in March, as Mr Burrells in Joan Temple's *No Room at the Inn*. Later became an actor-manager, running repertory seasons at Sidmouth, Ilfracombe, and various seaside resorts.

1950   *The Devil Inside Him*, written in collaboration with Stella Linden, staged at Huddersfield.

1951   June. Married Pamela Elizabeth Lane, an actress.

1955   *Personal Enemy*, written in collaboration with Anthony Creighton, staged at Harrogate. Apart from *Epitaph for George Dillon*, on which he also collaborated with Anthony Creighton, Osborne wrote two other plays, so far unperformed, before *Look Back in Anger*. He worked on this during a spell of unemployment, submitted it to the newly-formed English Stage Company, and had his script accepted within two weeks.

1956   April. Joined the English Stage Company as an actor. 8th May. First performance of *Look Back in Anger*. 15th May. Made his first appearance as an actor on the London stage, as Antonio in *Don Juan* and Lionel in *The Death of Satan*, at the Royal Court. Appeared at the same theatre in *Cards of Identity* in June, and as Lin To in *The Good Woman of Setzuan* in October. *Evening Standard* Award as Most Promising Playwright of the Year.

1957   10th April. First performance of *The Entertainer*. Appeared at the Royal Court as the Commissionaire in *The Apollo de Bellac* during May, and as Donald Blake in *The Making of Moo* during June. *Look Back in Anger* performed at the World Youth Festival in Moscow in July. Its New York production received the Drama Critics Award for the Best Play of 1957. August. Marriage to Pamela Lane dissolved. Married Mary Ure, the actress, on 8th November.

1958   New York production of *The Entertainer*, and London and New York productions of *Epitaph for George Dillon*. Founded Woodfall Films with Tony Richardson.

1959   London production of *The World of Paul Slickey*. Film of *Look Back in Anger* released, directed by Tony Richardson.

1960   6th November. Transmission of his only play for television, *A Subject of Scandal and Concern*. Film of *The Entertainer* released.

1961   London production of *Luther*, which also visited theatre festivals in Paris, Holland and Edinburgh.

1962   London production of the two *Plays for England*. *The Devil Inside Him*, written in collaboration with Stella Linden in 1950, staged at the Pembroke Theatre, Croydon, as *Cry for Love*, by Robert Owen.

1963   Marriage to Mary Ure dissolved. New York production of *Luther*, which received the New York Drama Critics Award and the Tony Award for the Best Play of 1963. Married the critic and journalist Penelope Gilliatt on 24th May.

1964   London production of *Inadmissible Evidence* opened in September. Appeared as Claude Hickett in the revival of *A Cuckoo in The Nest* at the Royal Court in October. Received the Film Academy's Oscar Award for his screenplay of *Tom Jones*.

1965   Directed Charles Wood's *Meals on Wheels* at the Royal Court in May. London production of *A Patriot for Me*, and New York productions of *Inadmissible Evidence* and of the *Plays for England*. *A Subject of Scandal and Concern* produced as stage-play in New York.

1966   London production of *A Bond Honoured* at the National Theatre.

1967   Marriage to Penelope Gilliatt dissolved: there was one child of the marriage, Nolan Kate.

1968   First London productions of *Time Present* and *The Hotel in Amsterdam*. Married the actress Jill Bennett.

Cast Lists

Look Back in Anger

Directed by Tony Richardson. Designed by Alan Tagg. First London performance at the Royal Court Theatre on 8th May 1956. This production transferred to the Lyric Theatre, Hammersmith, on 5th November 1956, and returned to the Royal Court Theatre on 11th March 1957.

Jimmy Porter	Kenneth Haigh
Cliff Lewis	Alan Bates
Alison Porter	Mary Ure
Helena Charles	Helena Hughes
Colonel Redfern	John Welsh

In the production at the Lyric Theatre, Hammersmith, the part of Jimmy Porter was played by Richard Pasco, that of Alison Porter by Doreen Aris, that of Helena Charles by Vivienne Drummond, and that of Colonel Redfern by Kenneth Edwards. In the subsequent production at the Royal Court Theatre the part of Alison Porter was played by Heather Sears, and that of Colonel Redfern by Deering Wells.

———

Directed by John Dexter. First London performance of this revival at the Royal Court Theatre on 28th October 1957.

Jimmy Porter	..	..	..	.. Alec McCowen
Alison Porter	..	..	..	.. Clare Austin
Cliff Lewis	..	..	..	.. Gary Raymond
Helena Charles	..	..	..	.. Anna Steele
Colonel Redfern		..	..	.. Willoughby Gray

Directed by Anthony Page. Designed by Tony Abbott and Donald Taylor. First London performance of this revival at the Royal Court Theatre on 29th October 1968. The production transferred to the Criterion Theatre on 10th December 1968.

Jimmy Porter	..	..	..	.. Victor Henry
Cliff Lewis	..	..	..	.. Martin Shaw
Alison Porter	..	..	..	.. Jane Asher
Helena Charles		..	..	.. Caroline Mortimer
Colonel Redfern		..	..	.. Edward Jewesbury

The Entertainer

Directed by Tony Richardson. Designed by Alan Tagg. Costumes by Clare Jeffery. Music by John Addison. First London performance at the Royal Court Theatre on 10th April 1957. This production transferred to the Palace Theatre on 10th September 1957.

Billy Rice	..	..	..	.. George Relph
Jean Rice	..	..	..	.. Dorothy Tutin
Phoebe Rice		..	..	.. Brenda de Banzie
Archie Rice		..	..	.. Laurence Olivier
Frank Rice	..	..	..	.. Richard Pasco
Britannia	..	..	..	.. Vivienne Drummond
William Rice		..	..	.. Aubrey Dexter
Graham	..	..	..	.. Stanley Meadows

In the production at the Palace Theatre the part of Jean Rice was played by Joan Plowright, and later by Geraldine McEwan, that of Britannia by Jennifer Wallace, that of William Rice by Albert Chevalier, and that of Graham by Robert Stephens.

Epitaph for George Dillon

Written in collaboration with Anthony Creighton. Directed by William Gaskill. Designed by Stephen Doncaster. First London performance at the Royal Court Theatre on 11th February 1958. This production, retitled *George Dillon*, transferred to the Comedy Theatre on 29th May 1958.

Josie Elliot	Wendy Craig
Ruth Gray	Yvonne Mitchell
Mrs Elliot	Alison Leggatt
Norah Elliot	Avril Elgar
Percy Elliot	Toke Townley
George Dillon	Robert Stephens
Geoffrey Colwyn-Stuart	Philip Locke
Mr Webb	Paul Bailey
Barney Evans	Nigel Davenport

In the production at the Comedy Theatre the part of Percy Elliot was played by Malcolm Hayes, that of Mr Webb by James Wellman, and that of Barney Evans by Stanley Van Beers.

––––––––

The first English performance of *Epitaph for George Dillon* was given by the Oxford Experimental Theatre Club, at the Commercial Road Hall, Oxford, on 26th February 1957, in a production by Don Taylor. The part of Josie Elliot was

played by Josie Chapman, that of Ruth Gray by Penny
Hopkin, that of Mrs Elliot by Mary Lee, that of Percy Elliot
by Donald Heighway, that of George Dillon by Bryan
Wright, that of Geoffrey Colwyn-Stuart by Noel Kershaw,
and that of Barney Evans by Frederick Mandle.

The World of Paul Slickey

Directed by John Osborne. Music by Christopher Whelen.
Designed by Hugh Casson. Costumes by Jocelyn Rickards.
Choreography by Kenneth Macmillan. Lighting by Michael
Northen. First London performance at the Palace Theatre
on 5th May 1959.

Copy-Boys	David Harding
	Julian Bolt
Telephonist	Norma Dunbar
Jo, the Secretary	Irene Hamilton
Jack Oakham, alias Paul Slickey	Dennis Lotis
Common Man	Ken Robson
First Naval Man	Ben Aris
Second Naval Man	Geoffrey Webb
Deirdre Rawley	Maureen Quinney
Lady Mortlake	Marie Löhr
Trewin	Aidan Turner
Michael Rawley	Jack Watling
Mrs Giltedge-Whyte	Janet Hamilton-Smith
Gillian Giltedge-Whyte	Janet Gray
Lord Mortlake	Harry Welchman
Schoolgirls	Pamela Miller
	Patricia Ashworth
Guide and Journalist	Geoffrey Webb
Photographer	Charles Schuller

Wendover	Ben Aris
George	Tony Sympson
Lesley Oakham	Adrienne Corri
Father Evilgreene	Philip Locke
Edna Francis-Evans	Jane Shore
Cornelia Tuesday	Anna Sharkey
Belgravia Lumley	Patricia Ashworth
Ida Merrick	Stella Claire
Terry Maroon	Roy Sone

Chorus of Journalists: Geoffrey Webb, Ben Aris, Julian Bolt, David Harding, Ken Robson and Charles Schuller. Stella Claire, Patricia Ashworth, Norma Dunbar, Pamela Miller, Anna Sharkey and Jane Shore.

A Subject of Scandal and Concern

Directed by Tony Richardson. Designed by Tony Abbott. First transmitted by BBC Television on 6th November 1960.

The Narrator	John Freeman
George Holyoake	Richard Burton
Mrs Holyoake	Rachel Roberts
Chairman	George Howe
Maitland	Colin Douglas
Mrs Holyoake's Sister ..	Hope Jackman
Brother-in-Law	Hamish Roughead
Mr Bubb	Donald Eccles
Chairman of the Magistrates ..	Willoughby Goddard
Captain Lefroy	David C. Browning
Mr Pinching	John Ruddock
Captain Mason	Ian Ainsley
Mr Cooper	Robert Cawdron

Mr Jones	..	..	..	..	Charles Carson
Jailer	..	..	..	..	John Dearth
Clerk to the Assizes		..	..	William Devlin
Mr Justice Erskine		..	..	George Devine
Mr Alexander	..	..	..	Nicholas Meredith
Mr Bartram	..	..	..	Nigel Davenport
Chaplain		..	..	..	Andrew Keir

Luther

Directed by Tony Richardson. Designed by Jocelyn Herbert. Music by John Addison. First London performance at the Royal Court Theatre on 27th July 1961. This production transferred to the Phoenix Theatre on 5th September 1961.

Knight	..	..	..	..	..	Julian Glover
Prior	..	..	..	..	..	James Cairncross
Martin	..	..	..	..	..	Albert Finney
Hans	..	..	..	..	..	Bill Owen
Lucas	..	..	..	..	..	Peter Duguid
Weinand	..	..	..	..	Dan Meaden
Tetzel	..	..	..	..	..	Peter Bull
Staupitz		..	..	..	..	George Devine
Cajetan	..	..	..	..	..	John Moffatt
Miltitz		..	..	..	..	Robert Robinson
Leo	..	..	..	..	..	Charles Kay
Eck	..	..	..	..	..	James Cairncross
Katherine		..	..	..	..	Meryl Gourley

Monks, Lords and Peasants: Stacey Davies, Murray Evans, Derek Fuke and Malcolm Taylor. Singers: John Kirk, Ian Partridge, Frank Davies, Andrew Pearmain and David Read. Children: Roger Harbird and Paul Large.

In the production at the Phoenix Theatre, the part of Staupitz was taken over by Carleton Hobbs.

Plays for England

The Blood of the Bambergs directed by John Dexter, and *Under Plain Cover* by Jonathan Miller. Both plays designed by Alan Tagg. Film sequence in *The Blood of the Bambergs* by John Dexter, Desmond Davies and Tony Gibbs. Music by John Addison. First London performances at the Royal Court Theatre on 19th July 1962.

THE BLOOD OF THE BAMBERGS

Wimple	James Cossins
Cameraman	John Maynard
Lemon	Billy Russell
Floor Assistant	Barbara Keogh
Brown	Glyn Owen
Taft	Graham Crowden
Withers	Anton Rodgers
Guards	Tony Caunter
	Jimmy Gardner
Russell	John Meillon
First Footman	Charles Lewsen
Second Footman	Norman Allen
Third Footman	John Maynard
Woman	Avril Elgar
Melanie	Vivian Pickles
Archbishop	Alan Bennett
First Reporter	Robin Chapman
Second Reporter	Barbara Keogh
Third Reporter	Tony Caunter
Fourth Reporter	Constance Lorne
Fifth Reporter	Jimmy Gardner

Postman	Billy Russell
Tim	Anton Rodgers
Jenny	Ann Beach
Stanley	Glyn Owen
First Reporter	Robert Eastgate
Second Reporter	Donald Troesden
Third Reporter	Robin Chapman
Fourth Reporter	Tony Caunter
Bridegroom's Mother	Constance Lorne
Bride's Mother	Avril Elgar
Bridegroom's Father	James Cossins
Bridegroom	John Maynard
Bridegroom's Brother	Norman Allen
Bride's Father	Jimmy Gardner
Waiter	Charles Lewsen
Guests	Barbara Keogh
	Pauline Taylor

Inadmissible Evidence

Directed by Anthony Page. Designed by Jocelyn Herbert. Sound by Marc Wilkinson. First London performance at the Royal Court Theatre on 9th September 1964. This production transferred to Wyndham's Theatre on 17th March 1965.

Jones	John Quentin
Bill Maitland	Nicol Williamson
Hudson	Arthur Lowe
Shirley	Ann Beach
Joy	Lois Daine
Mrs Garnsey	Clare Kelly
Jane Maitland	Natasha Pyne
Liz	Sheila Allen

In the production at Wyndham's Theatre the part of Jones was played by John Hurt, that of Hudson by Cyril Raymond, that of Joy by Coral Atkins, and that of Liz by Eleanor Fazan.

A Patriot for Me

Directed by Anthony Page. Designed by Jocelyn Herbert. Musical Director: Tibor Kunstler. Lighting by Robert Ornbo. First London performance at the Royal Court Theatre on 30th June 1965.

Alfred Redl	Maximilian Schell
August Siczynski	John Castle
Steinbauer	Rio Fanning
Ludwig Max von Kupfer	Frederick Jaeger
Kupfer's Seconds	Lew Luton
	Richard Morgan
Privates	Tim Pearce
	David Schurmann
	Thick Wilson
Lieutenant-Colonel Ludwig von Möhl	Clive Morton
Adjutant	Timothy Carlton
Maximilian von Taussig	Edward Fox
Albrecht	Sandor Eles
Waiters at Anna's	Peter John
	Domy Reiter
Whores	Dona Martyn
	Virginia Wetherell
	Jackie Daryl
	Sandra Hampton
Anna	Laurel Mather
Hilde	Jennifer Jayne
Stanitsin	Desmond Perry
Colonel Mischa Oblensky	George Murcell
General Conrad von Hotzendorf	Sebastian Shaw

Countess Sophia Delyanoff	Jill Bennett
Judge Advocate Jaroslav Kunz ..	Ferdy Mayne
Café Waiters	Anthony Roye
	Domy Reiter
Group at Table	Dona Martyn
	Laurel Mather
	Bryn Bartlett
	Cyril Wheeler
Young Man in Café	Paul Robert
Paul	Douglas Sheldon
Baron von Epp	George Devine
Ferdy	John Forbes
Figaro	Thick Wilson
Lieutenant Stefan Kovacs	Hal Hamilton
Marie-Antoinette	Lew Luton
Tsarina	Domy Reiter
Lady Godiva	Peter John
Flunkey	David Schurmann
Shepherdesses	Franco Derosa
	Robert Kidd
Dr Schoepfer	Vernon Dobtcheff
Boy	Franco Derosa
Second Lieutenant Viktor Jerzabek ..	Tim Pearce
Hotel Waiters	Bryn Bartlett
	Lew Luton
Orderly	Richard Morgan
Mischa Lipschutz	David Schurmann
Mitzi Heigel	Virginia Wetherell
Minister	Anthony Roye
Voices of Deputies	Clive Morton
	Sebastian Shaw
	George Devine
	Vernon Dobtcheff
	Cyril Wheeler

Officers, Flunkeys, Hofburg Guests and Ball Guests: Timothy Carlton, Lew Luton, Hal Hamilton, Richard Morgan, John Forbes, Peter John, Cyril Wheeler, Douglas Sheldon, Bryn Bartlett, Dona Martyn, Virginia Wetherell, Jackie Daryl, Sandra Hampton, Laurel Mather, John Castle, Edward Fox, Paul Robert and Tim Pearce.

A Bond Honoured

Directed by John Dexter. Designed by Michael Annals. Lighting by Richard Pilbrow. Musical Adviser: Marc Wilkinson. First London performance at the National Theatre on 6th June 1966.

Dionisio	Michael Byrne
Berlebeyo	Graham Crowden
Gerardo	Paul Curran
Lidora	Janina Faye
Tizon	Gerald James
Marcela	Maggie Smith
Leonido	Robert Stephens
Maid	Chloe Ashcroft
Zulema	Neil Fitzpatrick
Zarrabulli	John Hallam
Shepherd	Frank Wylie

Time Present

Directed by Anthony Page. Designed by Tony Abbott and Donald Taylor. Costumes by Ruth Myers. Lighting by Andy Phillips. First London performance at the Royal Court Theatre on 23rd May 1968. This production transferred to the Duke of York's Theatre on 11th July 1968.

Edith	..	..	..	..	Valerie Taylor
Pauline		..	..	..	Sarah Taunton
Constance	..	..	..	..	Katharine Blake
Pamela ..	..	..	..	..	Jill Bennett
Murray ..	..	..	..	..	Geoffrey Frederick
Edward ..	..	..	..	..	Tom Adams
Abigail ..	..	..	..	..	Kika Markham
Bernard	..	..	..	..	Harry Landis

The Hotel in Amsterdam

Directed by Anthony Page. Designed by Tony Abbott and Donald Taylor. Costumes by Ruth Myers. Lighting by Andy Phillips. First London performance at the Royal Court Theatre on 3rd July 1968. This production transferred to the New Theatre on 6th September 1968, and to the Duke of York's Theatre on 12th December 1968.

Porter	..	..	..	..	Anthony Douse
Gus	..	..	..	..	Joss Ackland
Laurie	..	..	..	..	Paul Scofield
Margaret ..	..	..	..	..	Isabel Dean
Annie	..	..	..	..	Judy Parfitt
Amy	..	..	..	..	Susan Engel
Dan	..	..	..	..	David Burke
Waiter	..	..	..	..	Ralph Watson
Gillian	..	..	..	..	Claire Davidson

In the production at the Duke of York's Theatre, the part of Laurie was taken over by Kenneth Haigh.

Bibliography

WORKS BY JOHN OSBORNE

PLAYS

Look Back in Anger, 1957.
The Entertainer, 1957.
Epitaph for George Dillon, 1958.
The World of Paul Slickey, 1959.
A Subject of Scandal and Concern, 1961.
Luther, 1961.
Plays for England, 1963.
Inadmissible Evidence, 1965.
A Patriot for Me, 1966.
A Bond Honoured, 1966.
Time Present and *The Hotel in Amsterdam*, 1968.

FILM SCRIPT

Tom Jones: a Screenplay, 1964.

ARTICLES

This list of contributions to newspapers and other publications is by no means exhaustive. It includes articles in literary journals of which good reference libraries are likely to carry runs, pieces which have been reprinted in readily accessible form, and a few less easily obtainable items which seemed of sufficient intrinsic interest to warrant recording.

"Sex and Failure", in *The Observer*, 20th January 1957. Reprinted in *Protest*, ed. Gene Feldman and Max Gartenberg, 1960, 269–71.

"The Writer in his Age", in *The London Magazine*, IV, May 1957, 47–9. Reprinted in *Casebook*, 59–62.

"They Call it Cricket", in *Declaration*, ed. Tom Maschler, 1957, 61–84. Extracts reprinted in *Playwrights on Playwriting*, ed. Toby Cole, 1960, 140–4.

"Introduction" to *International Theatre Annual*, II, ed. Harold Hobson, 1957, 9–10.

"Foreword" to *Look Back in Anger*, Evans Acting Editions, n.d., 2–4.

"Come On In: the Revolution is Only Just Beginning", in *Tribune*, 27th March 1959.

"The American Theatre", in *Encore*, VI, March-April 1959, 17–21.

"The Epistle to the Philistines", in *Tribune*, 13th May 1960. Reprinted in *Casebook*, 62–3.

"That Awful Museum", in *Twentieth Century*, CLXIX, February 1961, 212–16. Reprinted in *Casebook*, 63–7.

"A Letter to my Fellow Countrymen", in *Tribune*, 18th August 1961. Reprinted in *Casebook*, 67–9.

"The Pioneer at the Royal Court: George Devine", in *The Observer*, 23rd January 1966.

"On Critics and Criticism", in *Sunday Telegraph*, 28th August 1966. Reprinted in *Casebook*, 69–71.

"*The Entertainer*", in *Writers' Theatre*, ed. Keith Waterhouse and Willis Hall, 1967, 51.

"On the Thesis Business and the Seekers After the Bare Approximate", in *The Times*, 14th October 1967.

INTERVIEWS

In *The Playwrights Speak*, ed. Walter Wager, 1967, 90–109. An edited version of an interview given to John Freeman in

Face to Face, broadcast on BBC Television, 21st January 1962.
In *The Observer*, 30th June and 7th July 1968. An interview, printed in two parts, given to Kenneth Tynan.

WORKS ABOUT JOHN OSBORNE

BIBLIOGRAPHIES

Shirley Jean Bailey, "John Osborne: a Bibliography", in *Twentieth Century Literature*, VII, 1961, 118–20.
Helen H. Palmer and Anne Jane Dyson, "John James Osborne", in *European Drama Criticism*, 1968, 305–10.

These are useful mainly for tracking down references to reviews of the original London and New York productions of Osborne's plays, in periodical publications and in "quality" newspapers.

SYMPOSIA

John Russell Taylor, ed., *John Osborne: Look Back in Anger, a Casebook*, Macmillan, 1968.

This includes reviews of the first performance of *Look Back in Anger*, items by Osborne himself, and a selection of general critical assessments. Cross-references are given below for articles reprinted in the *Casebook*, to which the work's title has been abbreviated.

CRITICAL AND GENERAL STUDIES

The only reviews of particular productions included here are those of retrospective or tangential interest: for first-night notices, the two bibliographies cited above and (in the case of *Look Back in Anger*) John Russell Taylor's *Casebook* should be consulted.

Clive Barker, "*Look Back in Anger:* the Turning Point", *Zeitschrift für Anglistik und Amerikanistik*, XIV, 1966, 367–71.

A. V. Carter, "John Osborne: a Re-Appraisal", *Revue Belge de Philologie et d'Histoire*, XLIV, 1966, 971–6.

Alistair Cooke, "An Angry Young Man on Broadway", *Manchester Guardian*, 3rd October 1957.

B. Denning, "John Osborne's War Against the Philistines", *Hudson Review*, XI, 1959, 411–19.

Nigel Dennis, "Out of the Box", *Encounter*, XVII, August 1961, 51–3.

Vera D. Denty, "The Psychology of Martin Luther", *Catholic World*, CXCIV, 1961, 99–105.

A. E. Dyson, *"Look Back in Anger"*, *Critical Quarterly*, I, 1959, 318–26.

Richard Findlater, "The Osborne Career", *New York Times*, 29th September 1957.

Ronald Hayman, *Contemporary Playwrights: John Osborne*, Heinemann, 1968.

G. K. Hunter, "The World of John Osborne", *Critical Quarterly*, III, 1961, 76–81.

Roy Huss, "John Osborne's Backward Half-Way Look", *Modern Drama*, VI, 1963, 20–5.

Charles Marowitz, "The Ascension of John Osborne", *Tulane Drama Review*, VI, Winter 1962, 55–68. Reprinted in *Casebook*, 161–5.

Mary McCarthy, "A New Word", *Harper's Bazaar*, April 1958. Reprinted in *Sights and Spectacles*, 1959, 184–96, and in *Casebook*, 150–60.

John J. O'Connor, "The Three Faces of John Osborne", *Audience*, VI, Spring 1959, 108–13.

"Profile: John Osborne", *The Observer*, 17th May 1959.

Daniel Rogers, *"Look Back in Anger*—to George Orwell", *Notes and Queries*, IX, 1962, 310.

E. Gordon Rupp, "John Osborne and the Historical Luther", *Expository Times*, LXXIII, 1962, 147–51.

E. Gordon Rupp, "Luther and Mr Osborne", *Cambridge Quarterly*, I, 1965–6, 28–42.

Ian Scott-Kilvert, "The Hero in Search of a Dramatist: the Plays of John Osborne", *Encounter*, IX, December 1957, 26–30.

Alan Seymour, "Maturing Vision", *London Magazine*, V, October 1965, 75–9.

Alan Seymour, "Osborne V.C.", *London Magazine*, V, May 1965, 69–74.

Irving Wardle, "Looking Back on Osborne's Anger", *New Society*, 1st July 1965, 22–3.

Irving Wardle, "Osborne and the Critics", *New Society*, 16th June 1966, 22–3.

Samuel A. Weiss, "Osborne's Angry Young Play", *Educational Theatre Journal*, XII, 1960, 285–8.

John Whiting, "*Luther*", *London Magazine*, I, October 1961. Reprinted in *John Whiting on Theatre*, 1966, 37–44.

Katharine J. Worth, "Shaw and John Osborne", *Shavian*, II, October 1964, 29–35.

MISCELLANEOUS REFERENCES

Geoffrey Carnall, "Saints and Human Beings: Orwell, Osborne and Gandhi", in *Essays Presented to Amy G. Stock*, 1965, 168–77. Reprinted in *Casebook*, 129–37.

John Kershaw, "John Osborne: a Modern Romantic" and "*Look Back in Anger*: Language and Character", in *The Present Stage*, 1966, 21–41.

Laurence Kitchin, "Redbrick Luther" and "The Wages of Sex", in *Drama in the Sixties*, 1966, 185–91.

John Mander, *The Writer and Commitment*, 1961. Extract reprinted in *Casebook*, 143–9.

Allardyce Nicoll, "Somewhat in a New Dimension", in *Contemporary Theatre*, ed. John Russell Brown and Bernard Harris, 1962, 77–95.

John Russell Taylor, "John Osborne", in *Anger and After*, 1962, 39–57. Revised version reprinted in *Casebook*, 75–96.

George E. Wellwarth, "John Osborne: Angry Young Man?" in *The Theater of Protest and Paradox*, 1964, 222–34.

Katherine J. Worth, "The Angry Young Man: John Osborne", in *Experimental Drama*, ed William A. Armstrong, 1963, 147–68. Reprinted in *Casebook*, 101–16.